ECDL® Advanced 2.0

European Computer Driving Licence

Module AM6 - Presentation

Using Microsoft® PowerPoint 2010

Release ECDL273v1

Published by:

> CiA Training Ltd
> Business & Innovation Centre
> Sunderland Enterprise Park
> Sunderland
> SR5 2TA
> United Kingdom

> Tel: +44 (0) 191 549 5002
> Fax: +44 (0) 191 549 9005

> E-mail: info@ciatraining.co.uk
> Web: www.ciatraining.co.uk

ISBN: 978-1-86005-852-3

Important Note

This guide was written for *Microsoft Office 2010* running on *Windows 7*. If using earlier versions of *Windows* some dialog boxes may look and function slightly differently to that described.

A screen resolution of *1024x768* is assumed. Working at a different resolution (or with an application window which is not maximised) may change the look of the dynamic *Office 2010 Ribbon*, which changes to fit the space available.

For example, the **Editing Group** on a full *Ribbon* will contain several buttons, but if space is restricted it may be replaced by an **Editing Button** (which, when clicked, will display the full **Editing Group**).

First published 2010

European Computer Driving Licence, ECDL, International Computer Driving Licence, ICDL, e-Citizen and related logos are all registered Trade Marks of The European Computer Driving Licence Foundation Limited ("ECDL Foundation").

CiA Training Ltd is an entity independent of ECDL Foundation and is not associated with ECDL Foundation in any manner. This courseware may be used to assist candidates to prepare for the ECDL Foundation Certification Programme as titled on the courseware. Neither ECDL Foundation nor **CiA Training Ltd** warrants that the use of this courseware publication will ensure passing of the tests for that ECDL Foundation Certification Programme. This courseware publication has been independently reviewed and approved by ECDL Foundation as covering the learning objectives for the ECDL Foundation Certification Programme.

Confirmation of this approval can be obtained by viewing the relevant ECDL Foundation Certification Programme training material page of the website www.ecdl.org.

The material contained in this courseware publication has not been reviewed for technical accuracy and does not guarantee that candidates will pass the test for the ECDL Foundation Certification Programme. Any and all assessment items and/or performance-based exercises contained in this courseware relate solely to this publication and do not constitute or imply certification by ECDL Foundation in respect of the ECDL Foundation Certification Programme or any other ECDL Foundation test. Irrespective of how the material contained in this courseware is deployed, for example in a learning management system (LMS) or a customised interface, nothing should suggest to the candidate that this material constitutes certification or can lead to certification through any other process than official ECDL Foundation certification testing.

For details on sitting a test for an ECDL Foundation certification programme, please contact your country's designated National Licensee or visit the ECDL Foundation's website at www.ecdl.org.

Candidates using this courseware must be registered with the National Operator before undertaking a test for an ECDL Foundation Certification Programme. Without a valid registration, the test(s) cannot be undertaken and no certificate, nor any other form of recognition, can be given to a candidate. Registration should be undertaken with your country's designated National Licensee at an Approved Test Centre.

Downloading the Data Files

The data files associated with these exercises must be downloaded from our website. Go to *www.ciatraining.co.uk/data* and follow the on screen instructions to download the appropriate data files.

By default, the data files will be installed to **CIA DATA FILES \ Advanced ECDL \ AM6 PowerPoint 2010 Data** in your **Documents** library\folder (or **My Documents** in *Windows XP*).

If you prefer, the data can be supplied on CD at an additional cost. Contact the Sales team at *info@ciatraining.co.uk*.

Aims

To demonstrate the ability to use a presentation application on a personal computer.

To demonstrate some of the more advanced features using *PowerPoint*.

Objectives

After completing the guide the user will be able to:

- create and add slides of various kinds to a presentation
- change colour schemes and background effects
- use clip art and drawing tools
- manipulate images
- add animation, sound and video clips
- create and edit charts and flowcharts
- format text, bullets and fonts
- create links to other objects outside the presentation
- produce custom slide shows

Assessment of Knowledge

At the end of this guide is a section called the **Record of Achievement Matrix**. Before the guide is started it is recommended that the user completes the matrix to measure the level of current knowledge.

Tick boxes are provided for each feature. **1** is for no knowledge, **2** some knowledge and **3** is for competent.

After working through a section, complete the matrix for that section and only when competent in all areas move on to the next section.

Contents

Section 1
Preparation

By the end of this Section you should be able to:

Know how to Plan a Presentation

Consider how to Use Colour Schemes

Be Aware of Accessibility Issues

Use Background Colours and Effects

Bullet Levels

Create, Save and Use a Template

Work with Master Slides

Use A Word Processed Outline for Text

Insert Slides

To gain an understanding of the above features, work through the **Driving Lessons** in this **Section**.

For each **Driving Lesson**, read the **Park and Read** instructions, without touching the keyboard, then work through the numbered steps of the **Manoeuvres** on the computer. Complete the **Revision Exercise(s)** at the end of the section to test your knowledge.

Driving Lesson 1 - Design Considerations

◫ Park and Read

PowerPoint is a powerful presentation graphics application, which allows impressive presentations to be produced with ease. Presentations can be viewed on screen, on an overhead projector, on 35mm slides, or as web pages.

Whilst this guide describes techniques needed to produce and run successful presentations, some thought should always be given to the target audience. Consider how to put your message across: the tone will need to be different for each audience, e.g. it would not be appropriate to deliver a presentation created for children to a business audience, or vice versa. You should also be aware of the level of knowledge the audience has of the subject and pitch the presentation accordingly. Too much explanation of areas with which the audience is familiar may cause them to lose interest. Likewise, too little explanation for an audience with little or no subject knowledge may have the same effect. Consider too the cultural background of the audience and make the presentation fit.

Practical considerations are also important. How big is the audience? How big is the room in which the presentation is to be delivered? Is the layout suitable - will everyone be able to see the presentation? Is the lighting adequate? You may need a projector and a microphone in a large room. Things like background colour and text legibility become more important in these circumstances.

Plan the length of the presentation appropriately. How much time is available? It may be necessary to create a long or short version of the slide show. Make sure the presentation makes sense and that the slides run in a logical manner. Set the slide timings appropriately; allow enough time to get the points across, but don't ramble or you may lose the attention of the audience.

Visual impact is almost everything in a presentation; the graphics and text support the dialogue. You should be aware of the value of using pictures rather than too much text and charts rather than rows of figures. At the same time, don't use too many different background colours or effects, or complicated detail; a consistent design scheme makes the message much clearer. Make sure the slides are clear with adequately contrasting colours.

These aesthetic, practical and ethical considerations should be at the forefront when designing any presentation.

Driving Lesson 2 - Colour Schemes and Accessibility

▣ Park and Read

To some extent the final visual quality of a slide is a matter of opinion, but there are some guidelines which can be applied. Good use of contrast is important, but too much colour can distract the audience from the main focus of the slide. Avoid colour combinations that will make it difficult for people with colour blindness to see, i.e. red-green and blue-yellow.

There are other accessibility considerations, e.g. for anyone with visual impairment you may need to increase the size of fonts used. Indeed, for any audience limit the number of fonts used and remember that sans serif fonts are clearer and easier to read. Limit the number of animations and transitions used if you are presenting to an audience who may be visually impaired. Some people with cognitive or visual disabilities are unable to read moving text, or it can cause so much distraction that they are unable to read the rest of the page. Screen readers can't usually read moving text either.

Because of accessibility issues, a presentation may be intended to be viewed on the web. In this situation you must ensure alternative text is added to graphical objects, because if a screen reader is used, any image without alternative text will not be recognised.

It is normal practice to use **colour schemes** in slides. A colour scheme is a set of predetermined colours that is applied to specific areas of a slide. When a presentation is first created, a particular colour scheme is applied by default, but this scheme can be changed or a new one selected. Standard colour schemes are designed to compliment the design template of the presentation, but individual colours within a scheme can be amended.

⌐ Manoeuvres

1. Start *PowerPoint* and click the **File** tab.

2. Select **Open** and locate the data files supplied with this course (see page 4 - **Downloading Data Files** for the location). Open the presentation **Assessment**.

3. This presentation has a design template of **Artsy** applied. In **Normal View** the **Slides** pane shows the consistent appearance of the slides.

continued over

Driving Lesson 2 - Continued

4.   To change the colour scheme select the **Design** tab and click 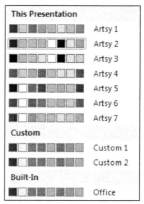 within the **Themes** group to display all available colour schemes.

5.   Move the mouse over the colour schemes to preview how the presentation will look.

6.   Right click the fifth scheme, **Artsy 5**, and select **Apply to All Slides**. All slides in the presentation change to the new colour scheme. The design template remains the same.

*The new scheme could be applied to the currently selected slide only by selecting the **Apply to Selected Slides** option. To maintain a consistent look to the presentation, however, it is recommended that all slides be changed.*

7.   To create your own colour scheme click the **Colors** button again and select **Create New Theme Colors**. A dialog box is displayed showing the individual colours that make up the current colour scheme.

8.   Select the colour box for **Text/Background - Dark1**, a **Theme Colors** drop-down chart is displayed.

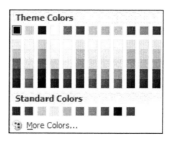

continued over

Driving Lesson 2 - Continued

9. Select a pale pink colour from the display.

10. Change the **Name** of the new colour scheme to **Training Needs Colour Scheme**.

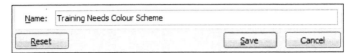

11. Click **Save**.

12. The new colour for **Text/Background 1** is applied to all slides, and is saved in the **Custom** section of **Colors**.

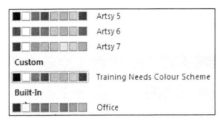

13. Click **Undo** 🔄 on the **Quick Access Toolbar** to undo the application of this scheme, although the new custom colour scheme still exists.

14. Make sure **Slide 1** is selected in the **Slides** viewer.

15. Click the **Colors** button.

16. In **Custom**, right click the **Training Needs Colour Scheme**.

17. Click **Apply to Selected Slides**.

18. The colour scheme is applied to **Slide 1** only.

19. Click **Undo**.

20. Leave the presentation open for the next driving lesson.

Driving Lesson 3 - Background Effects

▣ Park and Read

As well as colour changes, various other effects can be applied to the overall slide background. These can be applied to slides with or without design templates already in place, and generally they are more effective when applied to less cluttered slide designs. Effects that can be added are colour gradients, textures, patterns and pictures.

⌐ Manoeuvres

1. With the **Assessment** presentation open in **Normal View** select the **Design** tab and click [Background Styles ▾] from the **Background** group.

2. Move the mouse over the styles to preview them in the presentation, then click **Format Background**.

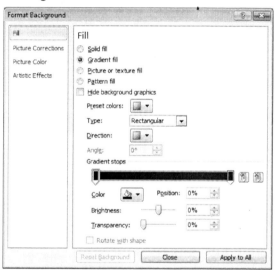

3. Make sure that the **Gradient fill** option is selected. Gradients can be selected from the **Preset colors** drop down box. Click **Preset colors** and move the mouse over the options to display their names. Select **Fire**.

4. Click **Apply to All** then **Close**.

ⓘ *Only the background of the slides changes. This can cause problems if a new background causes the content of the slides to be less visible, e.g. if a light background is applied behind light coloured text. Some trial and error may be involved to find a suitable effect.*

continued over

Driving Lesson 3 - Continued

5.   Open the **Format Background** dialog box again and select the option for **Picture or texture fill**.

6.   Click the **Texture** drop down box and move the mouse over each available texture - the name of each is displayed.

7.   Click on any texture to apply it. The effect can be previewed in the **Slides** pane.

8.   Any picture stored on the computer can be used as a background. With **Picture or texture fill** still selected, in the dialog box, click ⌊ File... ⌋ from **Insert from:**.

9.   In the **Insert Picture** dialog box, locate the supplied data files.

10. Select the **ostrich** file and click **Insert**.

11. With a picture background, existing graphics may not be appropriate. Select the option to **Hide background graphics**, then click **Apply to All**.

12. Close the **Format Background** dialog box.

 Pictures can be effective backgrounds and add an exclusive appearance to a presentation, but care must be taken. Pictures are more likely to distract attention from the slide contents.

13. Save the presentation as **Big Bird** and close it.

Driving Lesson 4 - The Slide Master

▣ Park and Read

Master pages contain text or graphics that are to be used on every page of a presentation. There are three types of master pages: **Slide**, **Handout** and **Notes**.

The main **Slide Master** allows uniform formatting, text or graphics to be added to every slide. A coloured or themed background may also be added. This will create a consistent look to the presentation. In addition, *PowerPoint 2010*, allows every different slide layout to have its own slide master if required.

⬧ Manoeuvres

1. Start a new, blank presentation. It should contain a single **Title Slide** with no data.

2. Select the **View** tab and click **Slide Master**. The slide master is now shown.

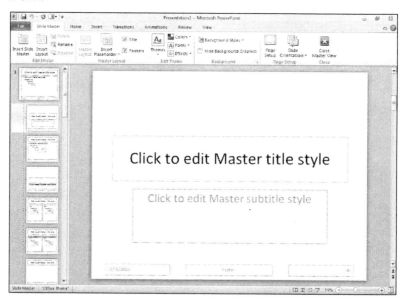

3. From the panel on the left, ensure that the top option is selected, the **Office Theme Slide Master**. This is the main master slide for all slides in the presentation. Any changes made here will affect the whole presentation and anything put on to this slide will appear on every slide.

continued over

Driving Lesson 4 - Continued

4.   Click in the text **Click to edit Master title style**.

5.   From the **Font** drop down list on the **Home** tab, select the **Arial Rounded MT Bold** font (use an alternative if this is unavailable).

6.   Change the size to **48pt**.

7.   Select the second text box: **Click to edit Master text styles**.

8.   Click on the top bullet's text and select the font **Arial Rounded MT Bold** but leave the font size as **32pt**.

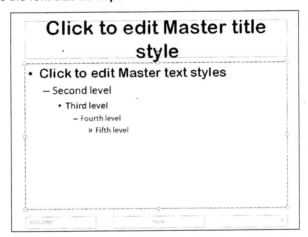

9.   Click on the edge of the **Footer Area** placeholder at the bottom centre of the slide master to select it and then press <**Delete**> to remove it.

10. Now click on the **Date Area** placeholder (lower left) to select it, then drag it to the top left corner of the slide.

11. From the **Slide Master** tab, select **Background Styles** and use **Format Background** to apply a **Gradient fill** effect to the slide master.

12. Select a **Linear** gradient type and the first **Linear Diagonal** option from **Direction**.

13. Under **Gradient stops**, set the **Color** to **Blue** from the **Theme Colors**, then click **Close**.

14. Leave the slide master open.

Driving Lesson 5 - Bullet Levels

🅿 Park and Read

Bullets are used to emphasise points in a slide. They can have many different types of symbols. In **Slide Master View** there are several levels of bulleted text available. This allows minor details to be made about major points. By default the bullet levels use the same style of font, etc. but the style can be changed for each level.

⤷ Manoeuvres

1.   The slide master should still be open. Notice that there are 5 bullet levels available.

2.   Click in the **Second level** bullet text and change the font to **Arial Rounded MT Bold**. Apply an italic effect. Leave the font size the same.

3.   To change the bullet character for the second level bullet, make sure the cursor is within the bullet text.

4.   Click the **Bullets** drop down list from the **Paragraph** group on the **Home** tab and select the first style on the third row.

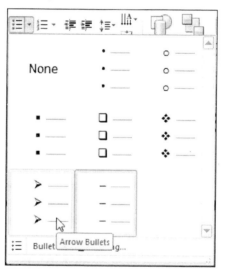

5.   Click in the **Third level bullet text** and change the font to **Arial Rounded MT Bold**, leave the size as **24pt**.

6.   Click the **Bullets** drop down list again and ensure the bullet character is the third style on the second row of the dialog box.

7.   Leave the slide master open and move on to the next Driving Lesson.

Driving Lesson 6 - The Title Master

▣ Park and Read

As well as the **Slide Master**, *PowerPoint 2010* provides master slides for every individual slide type. For example the **Title Slide Layout** controls the appearance of all **Title Slides** in the presentation. It allows you to create a different look for your opening slide in your presentation, or for any slides that may be used to introduce a new section in the presentation.

The slide master should be created first before changing the title master, as any formatting changed on the slide master also changes the title master.

Manoeuvres

1. The **Slide Master** should still be in the main area of the screen, click on the second slide from the top in the pane on the left, the **Title Slide Layout** master. The **Title Slide Layout** is now shown.

2. Click on the text **Click to edit Master title style** and change the font to **Broadway** (or some other distinctive font if this is unavailable).

3. Change the font size to **50pt** (you will need to type the size into the box and press **<Enter>**).

4. Click on the text **Click to edit Master subtitle style** and change the font to **Tahoma, 36pt**

5. Display the **View** tab and select **Normal** from the **Presentation Views** group.

continued over

Driving Lesson 6 - Continued

6. Display the **Home** tab and add 3 new **Title and Content** slides.

7. So you can identify the slides, add a title of **Title Slide** to the first slide **Slide 2** to the second slide, **Slide 3** to the third slide and **Slide 4** to the fourth slide. Notice the different fonts on the slides as defined by the master slides.

8. Custom slide masters can be added. Return to **Slide Master** view and insert a new slide master by clicking **Insert Layout**. The new master is called **Custom Layout** by default but it could be renamed.

9. This master is to be used by specific slides only. With the new master slide selected, apply the same fonts as on the default slide master, but make the background pale green.

10. Close **Master View**.

11. To apply this custom slide master to slide **4** only, right click on the icon for slide **4** in the **Slides** pane.

12. Select **Layout** from the shortcut menu. There is now an icon for the new custom layout in the panel.

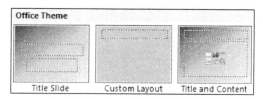

13. Click on the green **Custom Layout**. All formatting from this master is applied to the selected slide.

14. Click on each slide in turn in the **Slides** pane. Slide **1** has the **Title Master** applied, slides **2** and **3** the default slide master and slide **4** the custom slide master.

15. Insert a new slide at the end of the presentation and choose the **Title and Content** layout. The formatting from the **Title and Content** master is applied.

16. Save the presentation as **Custom Masters** and close it.

Driving Lesson 7 - Creating a Template

▣ Park and Read

Having spent considerable time and effort creating a suitable appearance for your presentation, you may wish to apply the same look to subsequent slide shows. Any layout can be saved as a **template** and then used as a basis for further presentations. This is particularly relevant for organisations, which often want a consistent corporate image for all their presentations.

Templates often contain only suitably formatted master slides so that any content can be added to create a presentation.

⌒ Manoeuvres

1. Create a new blank presentation with an empty **Title Slide**.

2. To create the template's style and background, select the **Design** tab and apply the built-in theme **Apex**.

3. Select the **View** tab, and click **Slide Master**. The left panel on the screen shows a general **Slide Master** for the whole presentation followed by individual master slides for each possible slide layout. Click on the first slide, **Apex Slide Master**.

4. Highlight the text **Click to edit Master title style**.

5. From the **Edit Theme** group select **Fonts** and change the font to **Georgia** (from the **Civic** theme).

6. Right click on the first bulleted line. Select **Font** from the shortcut menu. Select a **Font Color** of pale lavender then click **OK**.

7. On the **Slide Master** tab, select **Background Styles** from the **Background** group and select **Format Background** from the panel.

8. Select **Picture or texture fill** and select the texture **Medium wood** from the texture drop down list.

9. Because this effect is being applied to the **Slide Master**, it is automatically applied to every other slide (unless they are overwritten by effects applied by the theme) so there is no need to select **Apply to All**. Click **Close** to close the **Format Background** dialog box.

10. Right click on the first bulleted line and select **Bullets**.

continued over

Driving Lesson 7 - Continued

11. Select an arrow style bullet. With the cursor still in the first line, right click and select **Paragraph**.

12. Enter a **Line Spacing** of **Double**. Click **OK**.

13. Select the **Insert** tab, click **Picture** and insert the picture **safari.gif** from the supplied data files as a logo. Drag the picture to the lower right corner of the **Object Area**.

> **i** *The image is automatically applied to every slide master. If you wish to remove the image from an individual master then select the required master and from the **Slide Master** tab, check the box* ☑ Hide Background Graphics.

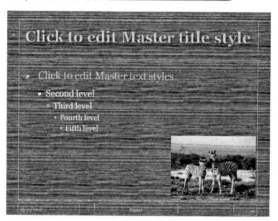

14. Click away from the picture and use the button on the tab to **Close Master View** and revert to **Normal View**. The layout of the slide is now ready to be saved as a template so that it can be easily used for other presentations.

15. Click the **File** tab and select **Save As**.

16. In the **Save As** dialog box make sure the **File name** is **Example** and select **PowerPoint Template (*.potx)** from **Save as type**. When this file type is selected the folder will automatically switch to **Templates**, the location of the existing *PowerPoint* templates. Click the **Save** button.

17. Templates can be stored in any location. Select **Save As** again. This time change the name to **Example2**. The file type should still be set to **PowerPoint Template (*.potx)**.

18. Use the **Navigation Pane** to locate the folder with the supplied data files and make this the destination folder. Click the **Save** button. This template is stored with the data files but will not be available automatically as a template when creating a new presentation in *PowerPoint*.

19. Click the **File** tab and select **Close** to close the presentation.

Driving Lesson 8 - Using a Template

◨ Park and Read

Once a template has been saved it can be used to set the appearance of future presentations. New presentations can be started with the design template or existing slides can be converted.

⌐ Manoeuvres

1. Click the **File** tab and select **New**.

2. Select **My templates**. As the **Example** template created in the last Driving Lesson was saved in the **Templates** folder, it can now be accessed. Notice that **Example2** is not available.

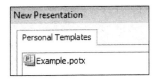

3. Select **Example** and click **OK**. A new presentation is created based on the **Example** template. On the blank title slide, enter **Example** as the title text and your organisation name as the subtitle text.

4. Click the arrow on the **New Slide** button and add a slide with the **Title and Content** layout.

5. Click to add a title of **Contents** and add two bulleted text lines of **Introduction** and **History**. Notice that all of the features defined when creating the template are being applied here, e.g. background, title style, bullet style, line spacing, logo image.

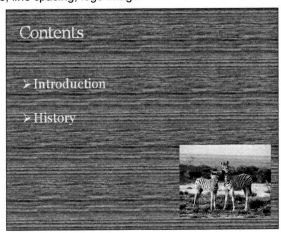

continued over

Driving Lesson 8 - Continued

6. Close the new presentation <u>without</u> saving and open the presentation **Assessment** from the supplied data files.

7. To apply the layout and colours of the template select the **Design** tab and drop down the **More** arrow from the **Themes** group.

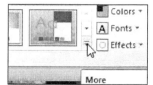

8. Click **Browse for Themes** and the **Choose Theme or Themed Document** dialog box is displayed.

9. Select **Recent Places** and locate the **Templates** folder in the list. Within the **Templates** folder, locate the **Example** template. Select it and click **Apply**.

10. All features of the layout are applied to all of the slides in the presentation. Display slide 2 in **Normal View** to see the effect more clearly.

i *Because the template is applied after the slides have been created there may be some conflict, e.g. Slide 4. It is usually better to start with the desired design and compose the slide contents to fit.*

11. To delete a template, follow steps 7 and 8 again and locate the **Example** template. Right click on the **Example** template.

12. Select **Delete** from the shortcut menu. Click **Yes** at the confirmation dialog box and the template is deleted.

13. Close the dialog box.

i *Any existing slides based on the template will not be affected.*

14. Close the presentation <u>without</u> saving.

Driving Lesson 9 - Inserting Text

▣ Park and Read

Individual sections of text can be imported into a *PowerPoint* presentation from word processing applications by using **Copy** and **Paste**. However, if a document is created with the correct styles already set up, it can be imported using a menu command in *PowerPoint* and will create new slides directly.

⌒ Manoeuvres

1. Open the word processing application *Word* and open the file **induction.docx**, which is included with the supplied *PowerPoint* files. Make sure **Outline View**, ▢, is selected from the **View** tab.

2. Examine the text; it has been formatted at different levels. When imported into *PowerPoint*, the highest level will be translated into slide titles, the next level into 1st level bullet points, and so on.

3. Close the document and close *Word*.

4. In *PowerPoint* create a new blank presentation. On the first slide, add **Induction** as the title text and your organisation name as the subtitle text.

5. Select the **Design** tab and expand the sample themes in the **Themes** group. Scroll down and apply the theme, **Verve** (or any other theme).

6. To import the outline select the **Home** tab, click the arrow on the **New Slide** button and select **Slides from Outline**. Look in the folder containing the supplied data files (make sure **All Outlines** is selected).

7. Select the file **induction** and click the **Insert** button in the dialog box.

8. Three new slides are created from the outline file, look at the **Slides** pane to see them all. Compare their structure with the original file layout (slide 2 is shown below).

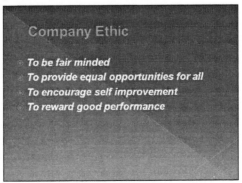

9. Save the presentation as **Induction** and leave it open.

Driving Lesson 10 - Inserting Slides

▣ Park and Read

Slides from existing presentations or even whole presentations, can be imported into the current presentation. In *PowerPoint 2010* this process is known as **Reuse Slides**.

⌒ Manoeuvres

1. View the **Induction** presentation in **Normal View** and select slide **4**, **Health and Safety**, from the **Slides** pane.

2. To reuse a slide, click the arrow on the **New Slide** button and select **Reuse Slides**. The **Reuse Slides** task pane is displayed.

3. Click the **Browse** button and select **Browse File**. Display the location of the data files.

4. Select the **Seminar** presentation and click **Open**. The **Reuse Slides** task pane is populated with the slides from the selected presentation.

5. Click **Slide 3**, **The Company**, to place the slide into the **Induction** presentation. There may be a delay as the slide is changed to match the design of the **Induction** presentation.

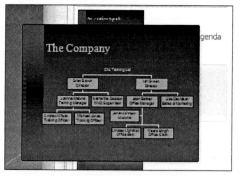

6. To insert more slides from a different presentation click **Browse** in the **Reuse Slides** panel (it should still be displayed). Select **Browse File** and open the **Extras** presentation.

7. Right click on any slide and select **Insert All Slides** to place all four slides of this presentation into **Induction**.

8. Close the **Reuse Slides** pane and view all nine slides in the **Induction** presentation, then **Save** and **Close** it.

Driving Lesson 11 - Revision

This is not an ECDL test. Testing may only be carried out through certified ECDL test centres. This covers the features introduced in this section. Try not to refer to the preceding Driving Lessons while completing it.

1.   After a presentation has been created, name 4 ways to present the final show.

2.   Is it good practice to give the same presentations to all audiences - why?

3.   What effect might slides with lots of different colours have on an audience?

4.   Why should care be taken when choosing colour combinations?

5.   What type of background effects can be applied to slides?

6.   Create a new blank presentation, add a title of **Tours** to the default title slide and apply a **Theme** of **Opulent**.

7.   Use **Slides from Outline** to create slides from the document **History**. The document is already in the correct format. Four new slides should be created.

8.   Add another slide at the end of the presentation by inserting slide **7** (the last slide) from the **Assessment** presentation. This becomes slide 6 in the new presentation. Is it necessary to change the design of the inserted slide?

9.   Save the presentation as **Tours** and close it.

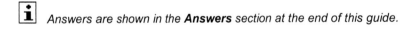 *Answers are shown in the **Answers** section at the end of this guide.*

If you experienced any difficulty completing this Revision refer back to the Driving Lessons in this section. Then redo the Revision.

Driving Lesson 12 - Revision

This is not an ECDL test. Testing may only be carried out through certified ECDL test centres. This covers the features introduced in this section. Try not to refer to the preceding Driving Lessons while completing it.

1. Open the presentation **Kittens**.

2. Apply a colour scheme. Select **Default Design 4** (it has a pale yellow background).

3. Click **Create New Theme Colors** to customise it. Change the colour of the scheme's **Text/Background - Dark 2** to blue and save the scheme as **Revision12**.

4. Change the background of all slides to a **Texture** effect of **White marble**.

5. Save the presentation as **Background** and close it.

6. Start a new, blank presentation. A template is to be created.

7. View the slide master and change the font of the **Title Style**, **Master text style** and **Second level** text to **Tahoma**.

8. Apply a **Linear** gradient background effect using an orange colour. Apply to all slides.

9. Save as a template named **Gradient** and close the presentation.

10. Create a new presentation based on the **Gradient** template. Create the following slides (use the <**Tab**> key to demote text to second level):

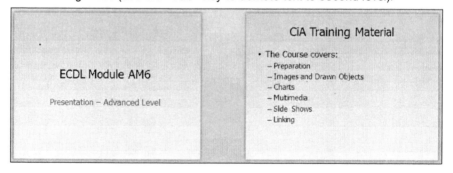

11. Save the presentation in the supplied data folder as **AM6** and close it.

If you experienced any difficulty completing this Revision refer back to the Driving Lessons in this section. Then redo the Revision.

Once you are confident with the features, complete the Record of Achievement Matrix referring to the section at the end of the guide. Only when competent move on to the next Section.

Section 2 Images & Drawn Objects

By the end of this Section you should be able to:

Work with Drawn Objects

Change Object Backgrounds

Rotate and Flip Images

Select and Manipulate Multiple Objects

Recolour Pictures

Crop and Edit Images

Save Images in Different File Formats

To gain an understanding of the above features, work through the **Driving Lessons** in this **Section**.

For each **Driving Lesson**, read the **Park and Read** instructions, without touching the keyboard, then work through the numbered steps of the **Manoeuvres** on the computer. Complete the **Revision Exercise(s)** at the end of the section to test your knowledge.

Driving Lesson 13 - Drawing Objects

▣ Park and Read

The **Shapes** function allows drawings to be created directly on to a slide. The **Drawing Tools** and **Picture Tools** tabs are only displayed when **Shapes** are inserted from the **Insert** tab.

Shapes can be drawn by clicking on the appropriate option and then clicking and dragging on the slide. All shapes have **handles**, that can be used to reshape and re-size the drawing. Once drawn, shapes can have various effects applied to them.

⌒ Manoeuvres

1. Start a new blank presentation and create a new, **Title Only**, slide and enter the title **Drawing**. If **Rulers** are not already visible, display the **View** tab and select **Ruler** from the **Show** group to help with sizing.

2. From the **Home** tab, click the **Shapes** button from the **Drawing** group.

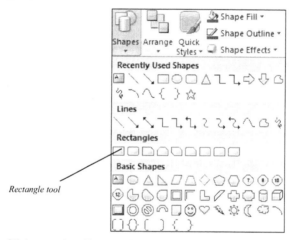

Rectangle tool

3. Click on the **Rectangle** tool to draw a rectangle about **5cm** wide anywhere on the slide.

ℹ *To set the size of a shape accurately, right click on it and select **Size and Position**.*

4. To change its colour click the drop down arrow on the **Shape Fill** button, 🔲 Shape Fill ▾ , and then select a green colour.

5. Move the coloured rectangle so that it obscures part of the slide title.

continued over

Driving Lesson 13 - Continued

6.   With the rectangle still selected (handles visible), click the **Shape Fill** drop down arrow and select **More Fill Colors, Standard** tab.

7.   Select a red colour from the grid and drag the **Transparency** slider to the right until **80%** is shown in the box.

8.   Click **OK**. The title can now be seen through the rectangle.

9.   Click on the drop down arrow on the **Shape Fill** button and select **More Fill Colors**. Change the figure in the **Transparency** box to **0**. Click **OK**.

10.   Drag the rectangle to the lower left corner of the slide so that hopefully it can be seen as the following effects are applied.

11.   With the rectangle selected, display the **Drawing Tools - Format** tab. Click the **Shape Effects** button within the **Shape Styles** group.

12.   Select **Preset** and move the cursor over the available options. Notice the effect on the rectangle. **Presets** apply a variety of different effects to the shape, including 3-D effects.

13.   To apply 3-D effects specifically, click **3-D Options**. The **Format Shape** dialog box is displayed with the **3-D Format** page shown.

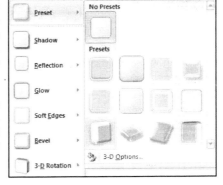

14.   Set the **Depth** value to **40pt**.

ℹ️   *The **Format Shape** dialog box can be displayed by right clicking the shape and selecting **Format Shape** from the shortcut menu.*

15.   Close the dialog box, click the **Shape Effects** button and select **3-D Rotation**.

16.   Move the cursor over the available options to see the effects. Click on **Isometric Top Up** from the **Parallel** options to apply that effect.

17.   Select **Shape Effects** then **3-D Rotation** and then **No Rotation** to remove the rotation effect and return the rectangle to its original form.

18.   Leave the slide open for the next Driving Lesson.

Driving Lesson 14 - Object Backgrounds

🄿 Park and Read

The range of background options available to slides can also be applied to drawn objects.

🄿 Manoeuvres

1.   Select the rectangle drawn in the previous Driving Lesson. To apply an effect click the drop down arrow on the **Shape Fill** button and choose **Gradient**.

2.   Hover the mouse over the available options and notice the various effects on the rectangle.

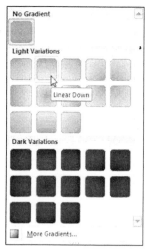

3.   Click **Linear Down** from the **Light Variations**.

4.   Insert a triangle shape next to the rectangle.

5.   Select **Shape Fill** then **Picture** and locate the data files. Select **Tower Bridge** and click **Insert**. The picture becomes the shape's background image.

continued over

Driving Lesson 14 - Continued

6. Draw an oval shape next to the rectangle, right click on the shape and select **Format Shape**.

7. Select **Fill** on the left of the dialog box, then **Picture or texture fill**.

8. Click the drop down arrow on the **Texture** option and select **Water droplets**. Click **Close** to see the effect on the drawn oval.

9. Resize and move the shapes until the slide is similar to the picture below.

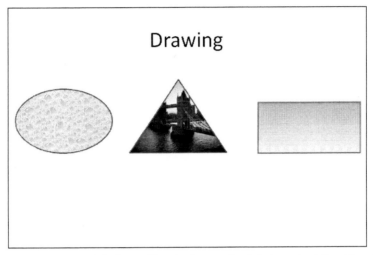

10. To apply the triangle's formatting to the oval, click to select the triangle then select the **Format Painter** button, 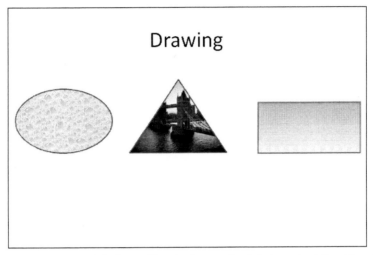, from the **Home** tab.

11. Now click on the oval. Click **Undo** to return the oval to its original format.

> ⓘ *To apply the same formatting to several objects, double click* 🖌, *then click on each object in turn. Click the button again, or press <Esc> to end the process.*

12. Right click on the rectangle. To make this particular gradient effect the default formatting for all new shapes, select **Set as Default Shape**.

13. Draw any shape on the slide. The red gradient formatting is now automatically applied to all new shapes.

14. Make sure the newly drawn shape is still selected and press <**Delete**> to remove it.

15. Delete the oval using the <**Delete**> key and leave the slide open for the next Driving Lesson.

Driving Lesson 15 - Rotating or Flipping Objects

▣ Park and Read

Any drawn object can be rotated or flipped. Objects on a slide can be manipulated individually or several at a time.

↷ Manoeuvres

1. Click on the rectangle to select it.

2. Move the mouse pointer over the green rotate handle of the object. Notice the pointer changes to ⟳.

3. Click and drag the handle from side to side. The rectangle is rotated about its centre.

4. Try rotating the object whilst holding down **<Shift>**. The object is rotated by 15° intervals rather than continuously.

5. Select the triangle. From the **Drawing Tools Format** tab select **Rotate** from the **Arrange** group. Click **Rotate Right 90°**.

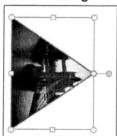

6. The triangle is rotated 90 degrees to the right. Select **Rotate Right 90°** again. The triangle will now be completely inverted.

7. . Select **Flip Vertical** from the **Rotate** menu. The triangle is now flipped over in a vertical direction so that it is now the original way up.

8. Try rotating and flipping the rectangle.

ⓘ *Flipping regular shapes like rectangles may not produce a visible effect. Try rotating the shapes slightly before flipping them.*

9. Return the objects to their starting orientation.

continued over

Driving Lesson 15 - Continued

10. Select the **Insert** tab, choose **Picture** and insert the **Butterfly** image from the supplied data files. Resize and reposition the images as shown in the picture below.

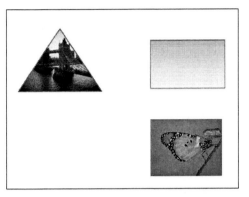

11. Click to select the rectangle. Hold <**Shift**> down and select the triangle and the image. All three objects should now be selected objects. Any formatting will now be applied to all objects.

12. Click one of the corner handles of the rectangle and drag it slightly outwards to enlarge the object. All the selected objects will be enlarged by the same amount. Click away to deselect them.

13. In the **Editing** group of the **Home** tab, click the **Select** button, ⬚, then **Select Objects**. Click and drag around the three objects. A rectangle appears until the mouse button is released. Any shapes wholly within the rectangle will be selected.

14. Rotate any object. All objects will rotate.

15. Return the objects to their original orientation and click away to deselect them.

16. Arrange them on the slide in roughly the positions shown below.

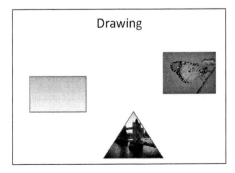

Drawing

17. Save the presentation as **Shapes** and close it.

Driving Lesson 16 - Recolouring Pictures

🅿 Park and Read

Various types of picture or drawn image can be added to a presentation and may then have background effects applied. It is also possible to recolour a picture; you may wish to do this so that it matches the theme/design template more closely.

🢖 Manoeuvres

1. Open the presentation **Theatre**.

2. View slide **3** in **Normal View**. The graphic on this slide matches the colour scheme quite well.

3. Check slide **4**; this graphic is OK too.

4. Move to slide **5**. This image is not really a match for the scheme.

5. Click on the picture to select it and make sure the **Picture Tools Format** tab is displayed.

6. From the **Adjust** group, click the [Color ▾] button.

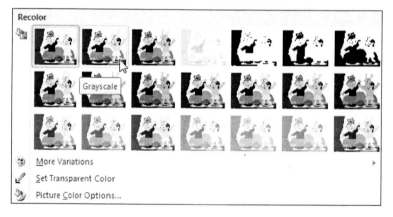

7. The **Recolor** options cover general recolouring. Click the second icon in this group (Grayscale). The picture is converted to shades of grey.

8. Click the **Color** button and then the **No Recolor** icon. The original colours are restored.

continued over

Driving Lesson 16 - Continued

9. Click the **Color** button again. Move the cursor over the various options in these sections to see the effect.

10. It is possible to recolour using non-theme colours. Move the cursor over **More Variations** to display a grid of possible colours.

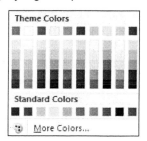

11. Click on **Red** from **Standard Colors** to apply this shade.

12. Click the **Color** button and then the **No Recolor** icon. The original colours are restored.

13. Close the presentation <u>without</u> saving.

Driving Lesson 17 - Converting Pictures

▣ Park and Read

Sometimes, before a picture can be manipulated, it must be converted to a drawn object, which means that its components are ungrouped into separate images. You may need to do this if you want to recolour a particular area of a picture not available otherwise. More can be done to change and enhance drawn objects than can be done to pictures.

⌒ Manoeuvres

1. Open the **Shapes** presentation created earlier and create a new **Title Only** slide. Add a title of **Conversion**.

2. Insert the **Clip Art** image shown here using the search **backpacker**. Enlarge the image to fit the slide.

3. The colour of individual parts of the image can only be changed if the picture is first converted. To convert the image, right click on it and select the **Group** from the shortcut menu and then **Ungroup**. The following prompt appears:

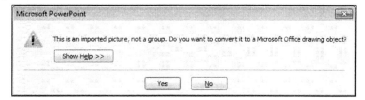

4. Click **Yes** to convert the picture. All component parts of the image are separated, or **ungrouped**. Click on the blue rucksack.

5. Notice the small handles around it. Change the fill colour to yellow.

6. Click away from the image.

ℹ️ *If you wanted to change the colours further, just click on the relevant part of the picture.*

7. Leave the presentation open.

Driving Lesson 18 - Background Graphics

▣ Park and Read

Graphics can be placed on the background of a slide using the **Slide Master**. However, this means that all slides would display the graphic. To apply a graphic to certain slides only, a setting must be applied to those slides on which the background graphics are <u>not</u> to appear.

☞ Manoeuvres

1. Using the current presentation insert three new **Title Only** slides. Name them **Slide 3**, **Slide 4** and **Slide 5**.

2. On the **View** tab, select **Slide Master**.

3. Select the **Title Only Layout**.

4. Insert the **Volleyball** picture from the data files onto the **Title Only Layout**. Drag the image to the bottom right corner.

5. Return to **Normal View**. The image will appear as a background on all **Title Only** slides.

6. Move to slide **3**. To stop the image appearing on this slide select the **Design** tab and check ☑ Hide Background Graphics in the **Background** group.

7. Note that the background image can detract from existing content such as the images on slide **1**. Hide the background image for this slide too.

8. Delete the graphic from all slides by selecting **Slide Master** then removing it from **Title Only Layout**.

9. Delete slides **3**, **4** and **5**.

10. Leave the presentation open for the next Driving Lesson.

Driving Lesson 19 - Arranging Objects

▣ Park and Read

Individual objects can be moved and resized by clicking and dragging, but there are also commands available to align and position them with more accuracy. A grid and ruler can be displayed to assist when moving objects around.

☞ Manoeuvres

1. Display slide **1** of the **Shapes** presentation in **Normal View**. The ruler and grids need to be displayed. Display the **View** tab and make sure the **Ruler** and **Gridlines** options are checked.

2. Right click on a blank part of the slide and select **Grid and Guides**.

3. The **Snap objects to grid** option automatically aligns objects with horizontal and vertical gridlines on the slide. Make sure this option is checked.

4. Click the drop down arrow in the **Spacing** box and select **2 grids per cm**. This produces a spacing of **0.5cm**.

🛈 The **Display grid on screen** option should be selected already.

5. Click **OK** to apply the settings.

6. Slowly drag the rectangle around the slide; notice how it "jumps" from one grid position to the next (you may need to zoom in to see this properly).

7. Right click on the slide and select **Grid and Guides**. Remove the check from **Snap objects to grid**. Click **OK**.

8. Move the rectangle and notice how it moves smoothly without jumping.

9. Reapply snap to grid, but uncheck **Display grid on screen** and change **Spacing** to **5 grids per cm**. Click **OK**. Move the rectangle to see the effect of the new grid settings.

continued over

Driving Lesson 19 - Continued

10. In the **Grid and Guides** dialog box, select the option to **Display drawing guides on screen**, then click **OK**. A horizontal and a vertical guide are displayed which divide the slide into four areas for layout purposes. Objects always snap to **drawing guides** if they are present.

11. Click and drag the vertical guide a few centimetres to the left and the horizontal guide a few centimetres downwards. The new layout will be available on all slides in the presentation.

12. Display the **Grid and Guides** dialog box and remove the check from **Display drawing guides on screen**. Click **OK**.

13. If you don't want to see the ruler, remove the check from **Ruler** in the **Show** group of the **View** tab. Display of **Gridlines** and **Guides** can also be controlled from here.

14. Shapes can be positioned more exactly on the slide. To specify the rectangle's position, right click on it and select **Size and Position** to display the **Format Shape** dialog box with the **Size** page on view.

*Alternatively, select the rectangle, display the **Format** tab and click the dialog box launcher, on the **Size** group.*

15. Select **Position**. Change the **Horizontal** position to **2 cm** and the **Vertical** position to **10 cm**. Leave both set as from **Top Left Corner**.

16. Click **Close** and the rectangle will be positioned exactly at that location.

17. Use any method to select all of the objects on the slide. With all objects selected and the **Drawing Tools Format** tab displayed, click **Align** from the **Arrange** group. Make sure **Align to Slide** is checked on the menu.

18. Click **Align** again and select **Align Bottom** from the menu. The objects are aligned with the bottom edge of the slide.

19. Click **Align** again and click **Distribute Horizontally**. The objects will now be evenly spaced across the slide.

20. For the same objects apply **Align Left**, then **Distribute Vertically**.

*If **Align Selected Objects** is selected instead of **Align to Slide**, the objects would be aligned and distributed only within the object group itself.*

21. Practise using the different aligning and distributing options from the **Align** menu to rearrange different groups of objects. Notice the difference when the **Align Selected Objects** option is selected.

22. Leave the presentation open for the next Driving Lesson.

Driving Lesson 20 - Cropping Images

▣ Park and Read

Whilst many of the same features can be applied to images and to drawn objects, there are some processes which can only be applied to images. One of these is **cropping**, when only a selected part of the image is required. The original image is still available.

↱ Manoeuvres

1. With the presentation from the last Driving Lesson still open, create a new, **Title Only**, slide and enter the title **Image**.

2. Select the **Insert** tab and click the **Picture** button. Insert the image **ostrich** from the supplied data files.

3. Click and drag the image to the lower left area of the slide. Click on the top right handle around the image and drag it diagonally up and right to enlarge the picture. Dragging a corner handle to enlarge an image maintains its correct proportions.

4. You need to crop the image so that only the head of the ostrich is displayed. Select the **Format** tab and click the **Crop** button from the **Size** group.

5. The picture is now surrounded by a cropping border and the mouse pointer changes. Move this pointer over the middle handle on the right edge of the image, ╟ and move it inwards. Release the mouse button. The picture will now be cropped.

6. Move the pointer over the middle handle on the lower edge of the image and drag it upwards, to crop the lower part of the picture.

7. Practise the cropping technique until only the ostrich head is displayed.

i *The cropping handles can be dragged outwards to reveal more of the picture if necessary.*

8. Click away from the image to remove the cropping cursor.

9. Leave the presentation open for the next Driving Lesson.

Driving Lesson 21 - Editing Images

▣ Park and Read

There are many commands on the **Picture** toolbar that can be used to alter the appearance of images on slides.

⌕ Manoeuvres

1. To return the cropped image from the last Driving Lesson to its original size and content, right click on the image and select **Size and Position**. Select **Size** from the left of the dialog box and click **Reset**. Close the dialog box.

2. Click and drag a corner handle to resize the image to about twice its original size.

3. Right click on the image, select **Size and Position**. Select **Size** from the left of the dialog box.

4. Notice how **Lock aspect ratio** is checked. This means that when **Height** and **Width** settings from **Scale** are changed, they change in relation to each other to maintain the proportions of the image.

5. Change **Height** to **100%**. Click in **Width** and notice that it has changed proportionally. Click **Close** to see how the image has been rescaled.

6. Display the **Size and Position** dialog box again and select **Size**. Uncheck **Lock aspect ratio**.

7. Change **Height** to **60%** and click **Close**. The image is now squashed, because it has been rescaled disproportionately.

8. Click **Reset** from the **Size** options to restore the picture to its original form.

9. In the **Adjust** group on the **Picture Tools Format** tab has several buttons to change the appearance of the selected picture. Click **Color**, ⟨Color ▾⟩, and move the mouse over the options in to preview them.

10. Select **Grayscale**. The image changes to the appearance of a monochrome photograph.

continued over

Driving Lesson 21 - Continued

11. Click **Color** again and select **Black & White 50%** to display the image in only those two shades.

12. Click **Color** again and select **Washout** to display the image as a watermark, which can be used as the background to other slide content.

13. To restore the picture to its original appearance, right click on the image, select **Format Picture**, select **Picture Color** from the left and then click **Reset** and then **Close**.

14. With the picture still selected, click **Corrections** | ☼ Corrections ▾ | from the **Adjust** group on the **Picture Tools Format** tab. Move the mouse over the icons to see the effects.

15. Click **Picture Corrections Options** and set the **Brightness** to 20% and the **Contrast** to -30%. Close the dialog box.

16. Right click on the image and select **Format Picture**.

17. Many image formatting operations can be controlled from this dialog box. **Fill** allows space in the image to be filled with colours or effects; **Line Color** and **Line Style** allows borders to be drawn around the image; **Shadow** and **3-D** allows the effects to be applied to the image frame; **Picture Color** has some of the recolouring and editing functions that can be found on the **Format** tab.

Fill
Line Color
Line Style
Shadow
Reflection
Glow and Soft Edges
3-D Format
3-D Rotation
Picture Corrections
Picture Color
Artistic Effects
Crop
Size
Position
Text Box
Alt Text

18. Select **Picture Corrections** and click **Reset**. Close the dialog box.

19. Create a new **Title Only** slide and name it **Transparency**.

20. Insert this **Clip Art** image using the search **pets**:

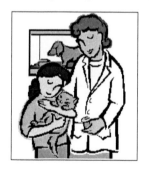

21. Enlarge the image then right click on it and select **Edit Picture**. A message is displayed.

continued over

Driving Lesson 21 - Continued

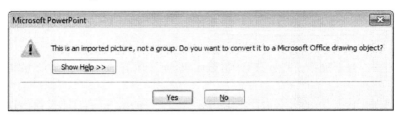

22. Click **Yes**. The image is converted. Now more editing options are available.

23. With the whole image selected, click on the vet's coat to select that element separately. Use the **Shape Fill** button to apply a yellow colour to the coat.

24. Click away from the image then click on it again to select the whole image. Press <**Delete**> to remove it.

25. One method of making any image partially transparent is to first use it to fill a shape. Display the **Insert** tab and add a rectangular shape. Make the shape about **4cm** wide and **5cm** high.

26. Right click the shape and select **Format Shape**.

27. With **Fill** selected on the left, select **Picture or texture fill**.

28. Click the **Clip Art** button and in the **Select Picture** dialog box, select the same image as before (use the search text **pets** again). Click **OK**.

29. In the **Format Picture** dialog box, drag the **Transparency** slide to about **70%**.

30. To remove the image border, select **Line Color** on the left then click **No line**. Click **Close**.

31. Drag the image so that it covers part of the slide title. The text will be seen through the image.

32. Leave the presentation open.

Driving Lesson 22 - Different Image Formats

▣ Park and Read

Images can be saved in various file formats. Some high quality images such as bitmaps have a larger file size than others. These will take much longer to display and this can be undesirable if the presentation is to be displayed on the Internet - download times will be longer. If an image is saved as a jpg, it will be displayed more quickly, it will make the overall file size smaller and it will still be of a good enough quality to use in your presentation.

⌁ Manoeuvres

1. In the current presentation, locate the slide containing the **ostrich** image.

2. Right click on the image and select **Save as Picture**.

3. Select the supplied data folder as the location for the save.

4. Change the file name to **ostrich2** and select **Device Independent Bitmap** from the **Save as type** drop down list.

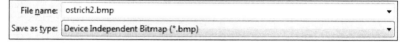

5. Click **Save**. The image is saved in a new format.

6. Select **Save as Picture** again and this time change the file name to **ostrich3** and the **Save as type** to **JPEG File Interchange Format**. Click **Save**.

7. Save the file again in **Portable Network Graphics Format (.png)** as **ostrich4**.

8. Use **Shapes** to draw a circle on the slide and make sure the shape has a **Fill** colour. Right click on it and select **Save as Picture**.

9. Save the object in **GIF Graphics Interchange Format (.gif)** format as **shape5**. Close the presentation <u>without</u> saving.

10. From the desktop or **Start** menu, display the contents of the **Documents** folder, and navigate to the data folder. Select **Details** view.

11. Notice the difference in size between the four versions of the ostrich file. The original image is a **.gif** file.

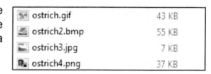

12. Close the **Documents** window.

There are many other applications available commercially to manipulate image files, and most of them allow images to be saved in a wide range of formats.

Driving Lesson 23 - Revision

This is not an ECDL test. Testing may only be carried out through certified ECDL test centres. This covers the features introduced in this section. Try not to refer to the preceding Driving Lessons while completing it.

1. Start a new blank presentation with a **Title Only** slide and enter the title **Drawn Objects**.

2. Draw a sun (**Shapes, Basic Shapes**), colour it yellow and apply any **3-D** format.

3. Draw a square and apply a green **Gradient** effect radiating from the centre of the square.

4. Draw a circle with a **parchment Texture** effect and apply any **Shadow** effect.

5. Set this effect to be default for all new objects.

6. Draw another circle and an oval.

7. Delete these last two objects.

8. Insert the following **Clip Art** image using the search **nature**.

9. Move or resize the other objects if necessary so that the image fits the slide and no objects overlap.

10. Convert the image to a drawn object.

11. What could you do to the image now that could not be done before it was converted?

12. Change the colour of the roof to red. This will involve several different sections of the image.

13. Save the presentation as **Drawn Objects** and close it.

i *Answers are shown in the **Answers** section at the end of this guide.*

If you experienced any difficulty completing this Revision refer back to the Driving Lessons in this section. Then redo the Revision.

Driving Lesson 24 - Revision

This is not an ECDL test. Testing may only be carried out through certified ECDL test centres. This covers the features introduced in this section. Try not to refer to the preceding Driving Lessons while completing it.

1.　Open the **Kittens** presentation.

2.　Select the image of the cat on slide **1**.

3.　Convert it to **Grayscale**.

4.　Now change it to **Washout** style.

5.　Move the image over the slide title.

6.　Right click the image and select **Send to Back** from the shortcut menu.

7.　Close the presentation <u>without</u> saving.

8.　Start an image editing application, e.g. *Microsoft Photo Editor* or *Paint*.

9.　Open the **cat** image from the data files.

10.　Save the file in **JPEG File Interchange Format** with the name **cat edited**.

11.　Save the file in **Portable Network Graphics** format with the name **cat saved**.

12.　Close the application.

If you experienced any difficulty completing this Revision refer back to the Driving Lessons in this section. Then redo the Revision.

Once you are confident with the features, complete the Record of Achievement Matrix referring to the section at the end of the guide. Only when competent move on to the next Section.

Section 3
Charts

By the end of this Section you should be able to:

Create Combination Charts / 2 Axes Charts

Edit and Format Charts

Create and Edit Flowcharts

Create Cycle and Pyramid Diagrams

Animate Charts

To gain an understanding of the above features, work through the **Driving Lessons** in this **Section**.

For each **Driving Lesson**, read the **Park and Read** instructions, without touching the keyboard, then work through the numbered steps of the **Manoeuvres** on the computer. Complete the **Revision Exercise(s)** at the end of the section to test your knowledge.

Driving Lesson 25 - Combination Charts

■ Park and Read

A **combination** (or **mixed**) chart shows different types of information by using two or more chart types. For example, a line-column chart may show projected figures as a column chart and actual figures as a line chart on the same grid. A **2 Axes** chart has a different axis on the left and right of the chart so that completely different data can be displayed on the same chart, e.g. rainfall and temperature.

Manoeuvres

1.   Start a new blank presentation.

2.   Change the layout to **Title and Content** slide and add the title **Sales Figures**.

3.   Click the chart icon to open the **Insert Chart** dialog box.

4.   Click **OK** to create the chart with the default **Clustered Column** format.

5.   The datasheet will appear on the right. Amend the values to those shown below, including reducing the range to two rows.

	A	B	C	D	E	F
1		Week 1	Week 2	Week 3	Week 4	Week 5
2	Sales Value	25000	23000	18900	20500	24000
3	Units Sold	1200	1000	750	1000	1150

6.   If the resulting chart does not look like the picture below, click the **Switch Row/Column** button on the **Design** tab.

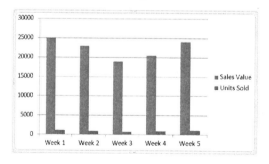

continued over

Driving Lesson 25 - Continued

7. Close the datasheet window and resize the *PowerPoint* window if required.

8. The units for **Sales Value** (currency) and **Units Sold** (numbers) are quite different, so a 2 axes chart is required to compare the figures. Right click in one of the red data columns and select **Format Data Series**.

9. In the **Series Options** pane of the **Format Data Series** dialog box set the option to plot the series on a **Secondary Axis**.

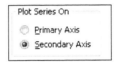

10. Click **Close**. Now the red data series is plotted using a new axis on the right of the chart. The data is still confusing. Right click in a red data column and select **Change Series Chart Type**.

11. Select the basic **Line** chart from the **Change Chart Type** dialog box and click **OK**. The **Units Sold** data is now represented by a line on the chart.

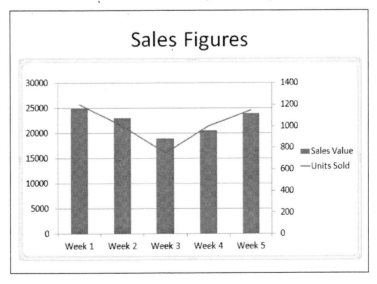

12. The axis for the **Sales Value** figures (blue columns) is on the left and is called the **Value Axis**. The axis for the **Units Sold** figures (red line) is on the right and is called the **Secondary Value Axis**.

13. Save the presentation as **Charts** and leave it open.

Driving Lesson 26 - Editing Charts

▣ Park and Read

Charts can be edited to show data in different ways. The type of the whole chart or a single data series on the chart can be changed; the scale of the value axis and the interval between the plotted numbers can be amended. The way figures are displayed can also be changed. Labels and legends can be formatted.

☞ Manoeuvres

1. With the **Charts** presentation still open, right click the **Sales Value** axis and select **Format Axis**.

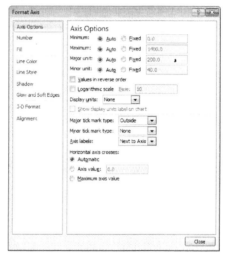

2. No figures below 18900 are displayed, so the lowest figure on the **Value Axis** can be changed. Change the figure in **Minimum** to **10000** by clicking **Fixed** and amending the value.

3. Change the **Maximum** value to **25000**.

4. The interval between each value on the axis is currently set at **5000**. Change the **Major unit** to **2500**.

5. To change the **Sales Value** units to thousands without amending the datasheet, click the drop down arrow next to **Display units**.

6. Select **Thousands**. There are many different values available - millions and other values can be used. Click **Close**.

7. With the axis still selected, change the font colour to blue (either use the **Home** tab or right click and use the shortcut formatting bar).

continued over

Driving Lesson 26 - Continued

8. Select the secondary axis on the right and make sure the **Chart Tools Format** tab is displayed. Click **Format Selection** from the **Current Selection** group as another way of displaying **Format Axis**.

9. Change the **Minimum** to **600**, the **Major Unit** to **100**, and the **Display units** to **Hundreds**. Change the font colour to red.

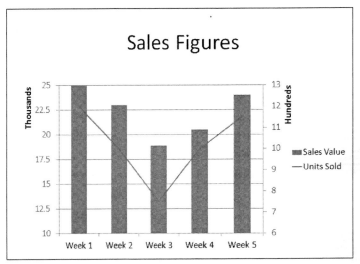

10. Display the **Chart Tools Layout** tab and click **Chart Title**. Select **Above Chart** from the options to add a chart title.

11. Change the title text to **Period 1** and change the font to **Tahoma**.

12. With the title still selected click **Format Selection** from the tab. Apply a solid fill of pale blue to the title. Do not close the **Format Chart Title** dialog box.

13. Click on the chart legend. The dialog box will change to **Format Legend**. Apply the same pale blue solid fill. Close the dialog box.

14. With the legend still selected change the font to **Tahoma**.

15. Click on a blue column to select the **Sales Value** data series. Display the **Chart Tools Layout** tab and click **Data Labels**.

16. Select **Outside End** from the options to add a data labels to the columns.

17. Click on a data label to select them all, then change the font to **Tahoma, Italic**.

18. Select the **Value Axis** label (**Thousands**) and change the font to **Tahoma**, again using either the **Home** tab or right click and use the shortcut formatting bar.

continued over

Driving Lesson 26 - Continued

19. Repeat this for the **Horizontal (Category) Axis** labels (**Week1**, etc.).

20. Pictures can be applied to various areas on a chart. With the chart selected, display the **Chart Tools Format** tab. In the top left of the tab, in the **Current Selection** group, is a **Chart Elements** box.

21. Click the drop down arrow to show a list of the available chart elements. Select **Chart Area**. This is an alternative way of selecting a specific chart element.

22. Click **Format Selection** from the tab. Make sure **Fill** is selected and click **Picture or texture fill**.

23. Click **File** under **Insert from** and select the file **Bridge** from the supplied data files. Click **Insert**.

24. With the **Format Chart Area** dialog box still open, click on the **Plot Area** of the chart. It may be necessary to move the dialog box first.

25. In the **Format Plot Area** dialog box, select **Picture or text fill** again. Click **File** under **Insert from** and select the file **pink and blue** from the supplied data files. Click **Insert**.

26. Click in one of the data columns. The **Format Data Series** dialog box is displayed.

27. Make sure **Fill** is selected and click **Picture or texture fill**.

28. Click **File** under **Insert from** and select the file **cat** from the supplied data files. Click **Insert**.

29. Select the **Stack** option.

 *Pictures are applied to bars in bar charts in the same way.*

30. This is quite confusing visually. Change the **Sales Value** data series back to a blue solid fill and click **Close**.

31. The **Sales Value** data series should be selected, if not select it now. To change the chart type for the **Sales Value** data series only, display the **Chart Tools Design** tab and click **Change Chart Type**.

32. Select the first of the **Line Chart** options and click **OK**. Now both data series are shown as line charts.

continued over

Driving Lesson 26 - Continued

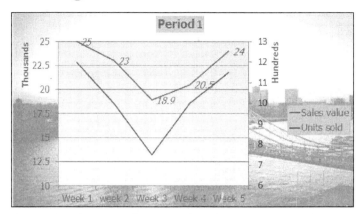

33. To change the chart type for the entire chart, make sure that no data series is selected and click **Change Chart Type** from the **Chart Tools Design** tab.

34. Select the first of the **Column Chart** options and click **OK**.

35. The new chart has only one vertical axis starting at **10 Thousand** and the **Units Sold** data is not seen. Display the **Format Axis** dialog box and with **Axis Options** selected, set the **Minimum** value back to **0**. Click **Close**.

36. Click on any data column and click **Format Selection** from the **Chart Tools Format** tab.

37. With **Series Options** selected, drag the **Gap Width** slider down to about 40%. All data columns become wider.

38. Drag the **Series Overlap** slider up to about 40% then click **Close**. All data columns now overlap.

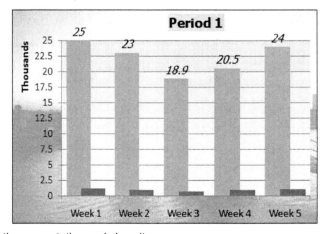

39. Save the presentation and close it.

Driving Lesson 27 - Animating Charts

▣ Park and Read

Charts can be animated so that the information is displayed gradually in a specified order.

⌐ Manoeuvres

1. Open the **Chart Test** presentation and select the chart.

2. To animate the chart select the **Animations** tab and click **More** button from the **Animation** group to display more options.

3. Select **Wipe**.

4. Click the dialog box launch button on the **Animation** group.

5. Select the **Chart Animation** tab in the dialog box for this animation effect.

6. From the **Group chart** drop down list select **By Category**. Make sure the **chart background** option is checked.

    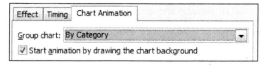

7. Click **OK** then run the slide show. A mouse click is required to display the chart background, then each further click displays another category.

8. End the slide show. Click the **Animation** dialog box launcher again and display **Chart Animation**. To change the order in which the data is animated, change **Group chart** to **By Series**. Uncheck the **chart background** option and click **OK**.

9. Run the slide show. Now the background appears automatically and each click displays a complete data series. End the slide show.

10. Click the **Effect Options** button. Change **Sequence** to **By Element in Series** and run the slide show again. Now the background appears automatically and each click displays a single column in a data series.

11. End the slide show, save the presentation and close it.

Driving Lesson 28 - Creating a Flowchart

▣ Park and Read

Flowcharts on slides can be created by combining preset **Shapes** available within *PowerPoint*.

⌐ Manoeuvres

1.   Start a new presentation. Change the layout of the first slide to **Title Only** and name it **Flowchart**.

2.   Select the **Home** tab and choose **Shapes** from the **Drawing** group.

3.   Select the **Flowchart: Terminator** shape, ▱.

4.   To start the flowchart click and drag the shape at the top left of the slide and type in **Order Received**. Flowchart shapes can be moved, resized and coloured like any other drawn object.

5.   Beneath this shape draw a **Flowchart: Decision** shape, ◇ and type **New Customer?**

6.   Complete the flowchart as below, using **Decision**, **Process** and **Terminator** shapes. **Centring guidelines** will appear to help position the shapes correctly. Press <**Enter**> to start a new line where necessary when typing text.

7.   With no drawing tool selected, click and drag around all the shapes to select them. Click the **Quick Styles** button from the **Drawing** group and apply a different style. The style used here is **Subtle Effect - Accent 1**.

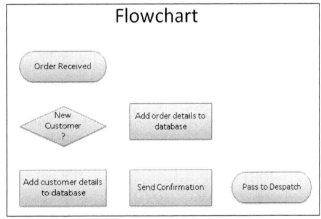

8.   To connect the shapes, select the basic **Arrow** shape from the **Lines** section of **Shapes**. The cursor on the slide becomes a cross.

continued over

Driving Lesson 28 - Continued

9. Notice how red handles appear as the mouse is moved over the shapes. Click on the bottom centre handle of the **Order Received** shape to start the connection.

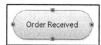

10. Drag the other end of the connector to the **New Customer?** shape. Red handles will appear on that shape. Drag the line to the top red handle, the line will 'snap' into place when it is close to the correct location. Release the mouse button to anchor the line.

11. When the connector has red handles at each end, it is locked to the shapes. Move the **New Customer?** shape to the left. The connector will follow it. Return the shape to its original position.

12. In a similar way, use the **Elbow Arrow Connector** to join **New Customer?** to **Add order details to database**.

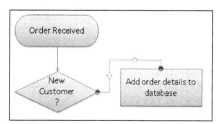

13. Join the other shapes as below

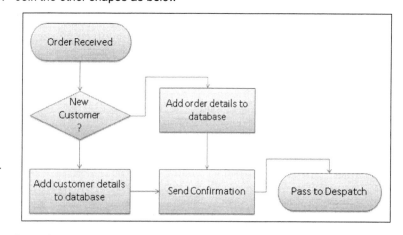

14. Save the presentation as **Flowchart** and leave it open.

*Flowcharts can also be created using other applications and then used in PowerPoint. A flowchart can be created and saved in Visio for example, and then imported into PowerPoint using the **Insert Object** command. This object can then be edited using Visio from within PowerPoint by double clicking on it.*

Driving Lesson 29 - Amending a Flowchart

▣ Park and Read

The shape and position of components used in a flowchart can be changed or deleted as necessary.

⌐ Manoeuvres

1. Using the flowchart created in the previous Driving Lesson, add a new terminator shape beneath **Pass to Despatch** and type in **End**.

2. The **Pass to Despatch** shape is the wrong type. Delete it by selecting the shape (not the text) and then pressing <**Delete**>.

3. Insert a **Flowchart: Predefined Process** shape, ▭ in the gap and type in the text **Pass to Despatch**. Connect it to the **End** shape with a **Straight Arrow Connector**.

4. To update the formatting on the new shapes, select one of the shapes formatted earlier. Click the **Format Painter** button ◿ and then click on the **Pass to Despatch** shape. Repeat this process to format the **End** shape.

5. Delete the connector between **Add customer details** and **Send Confirmation** by clicking on it and then pressing <**Delete**>.

6. Join the right edge of **Add customer details** to the top of **Send Confirmation** using an **Elbow Arrow Connector**.

7. Select the connector just added and drag the red handle at the right end of the connector up to the top of **Add order details** as shown below:

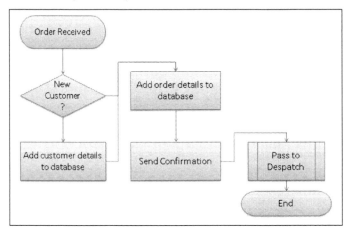

8. Save the presentation and close it.

Driving Lesson 30 - Creating Other Diagrams

⊞ Park and Read

PowerPoint helps you create various diagrams to help explain concepts in your presentation. Types available include **cycle diagrams**, which show the circular relationships between related processes, and **pyramid diagrams**, which are divided into horizontal slices to represent a hierarchy.

⌒ Manoeuvres

1. Open the presentation **Theatre** and insert a new **Title and Content** slide at the end.

2. Add the title **Workshop Teaching Cycle**.

3. Click the **Insert SmartArt Graphic** icon, [⊞], to display the **Choose a SmartArt Graphic** dialog box.

4. Select **Cycle** from the left and select the first option (**Basic Cycle**).

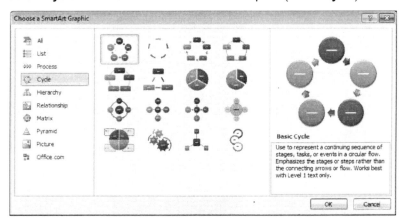

5. Click **OK**.

6. The first circular component of the **Cycle** diagram is selected. Type the text **Practise and Learn**.

7. Select the next circular area (clockwise) and enter **Test**.

8. Select the next circular area (clockwise) and enter **Assess**.

9. Click on the remaining circular areas in turn and press <**Delete**> to remove them.

continued over

Driving Lesson 30 - Continued

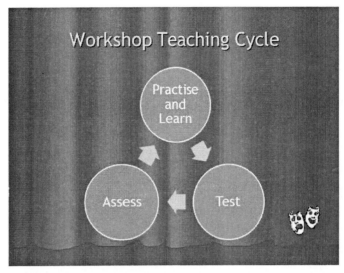

10. Insert a new **Title and Content** slide after slide **2** and add the title **Organisation**.

11. Click **Insert SmartArt Graphic** and select the first **Basic Pyramid** option. Click **OK**.

12. On the bottom level enter **Support Staff**, on the middle level enter **Administration**, and on the top level enter **Director**.

13. Display the **SmartArt Tools Design** tab and select one of the **SmartArt Styles**.

14. Click the **Change Colors** button and select one of the colour schemes from the **Colorful** range.

15. Click on the **Director** level and click the drop down arrow on **Add Shape** from the **Create Graphic** group.

16. Select **Add Shape After**. A new shape is added. Type in **Management**.

17. To remove it, click on the shape (not the text) and press <**Delete**>.

18. Click on the top shape in the pyramid (so that the cursor is a four-way arrow) and drag it to the right. Drag the second shape to the left.

19. Right click on the top shape and select **Reset Shape** to return it to its original position. Click **Reset Graphic** on the **SmartArt Tools Design** tab to restore the whole diagram to its original formatting.

i *Manipulating shapes is similar in all types of diagram.*

20. Save the presentation as **Theatre2** and close it.

Driving Lesson 31 - Revision

This is not an ECDL test. Testing may only be carried out through certified ECDL test centres. This covers the features introduced in this section. Try not to refer to the preceding Driving Lessons while completing it.

1. Open the **Assessment** presentation.

2. At the end of the presentation insert a new **Title and Content** slide and add a title of **Pass Rates**.

3. Add a **Clustered Column** chart and amend the datasheet as below.

	A	B	C	D	E
1		1st Quarter	2nd Quarter	3rd Quarter	4th Quarter
2	Estimated	80.5	85	90	86.5
3	Actual	93	91.25	87	97

4. Make sure the chart has this layout.

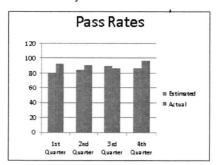

5. Close the datasheet.

6. Change the **Actual** data series to be a line chart.

7. Change the **Minimum** scale to **70** and the **Maximum** scale to **100**.

8. Animate the chart to introduce elements **By Category** with the effect **Wipe, (From Left)**.

9. Save the presentation as **Revision31**.

10. View the slide show for this slide and use the mouse button to introduce each section of the chart.

11. Close the presentation.

If you experienced any difficulty completing this Revision refer back to the Driving Lessons in this section. Then redo the Revision.

Driving Lesson 32 - Revision

This is not an ECDL test. Testing may only be carried out through certified ECDL test centres. This covers the features introduced in this section. Try not to refer to the preceding Driving Lessons while completing it.

1. Start a new blank presentation.

2. On a blank slide, create the flowchart with the content as shown below. Format the diagram in any way you like.

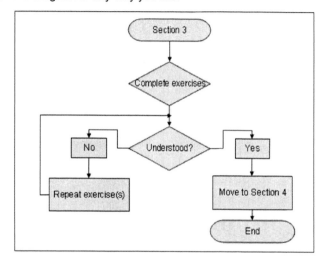

3. The **Complete exercises** shape should be a **Process** shape. Change it.

4. Add a new slide with a title of **Pyramid** and create a pyramid diagram with 3 levels.

5. The bottom level is **Learn**, then **Practise**, then **Understand**.

6. Format the diagram in any way you like.

7. Save the presentation as **Revision32**.

8. Close it.

If you experienced any difficulty completing this Revision refer back to the Driving Lessons in this section. Then redo the Revision.

Once you are confident with the features, complete the Record of Achievement Matrix referring to the section at the end of the guide. Only when competent move on to the next Section.

Section 4
Multimedia

By the end of this Section you should be able to:

Insert Sounds and Movies

Change Animation Settings

Change Animation Sequence

To gain an understanding of the above features, work through the **Driving Lessons** in this **Section**.

For each **Driving Lesson**, read the **Park and Read** instructions, without touching the keyboard, then work through the numbered steps of the **Manoeuvres** on the computer. Complete the **Revision Exercise(s)** at the end of the section to test your knowledge.

Driving Lesson 33 - Inserting Sounds

▣ Park and Read

A sound can be inserted on to a slide and will then play when that slide is viewed in the slide show. An audio track from a CD can also be inserted.

℞ Manoeuvres

1. Open the presentation **Holiday Choice** and move to slide **2**.

2. To insert a sound, display the **Insert** tab, and click the drop down arrow on the **Audio** button from **Media**. Select **Audio from File**.

3. Navigate to **(C:)/Windows/Media** and select the **chord.wav** file (this is an example of a sound file, any **.wav** file will do). Click **Insert**.

4. The sound is added to the slide and is shown as an icon.

5. Display the **Audio Tools Playback** tab. From the **Audio Options** group, click the drop down arrow from the **Start** options and select **Automatically**.

6. Click the **Slide Show** tab and choose to play **From Beginning**. The sound will play when the slide **2** appears. Notice the sound icon is still shown on the slide. Press <**Esc**> to end the show.

7. To control when the sound will play, make sure the sound icon is selected and click the **Animations** tab.

8. In the **Timing** group, set the **Start** to **After Previous** with a **Delay** of 5 seconds.

▶ Start:	After Previous ▾
☉ Duration:	00.64 ⬍
⏱ Delay:	05.00 ⬍
	Timing

9. Click the **Slide Show** tab. Select **From Current Slide**. Slide **2** will appear and 5 seconds later the sound will play. Press <**Esc**> to end the show.

10. Make sure the sound icon on slide **2** is selected and click the **Audio Tools Playback** tab.

11. Select **On Click** from the **Start** options drop down list.

12. Run the slide show again. Now the sound on slide **2** will not be heard until the mouse is clicked. Press <**Esc**> to end the show.

13. Make sure the sound icon on slide **2** is selected and the **Audio Tools Playback** tab is displayed. Select **Automatically** from the **Start** options drop down list.

14. To stop the sound icon appearing on the slide click the **Hide During Show** option from the **Audio Options** group.

continued over

Driving Lesson 33 - Continued

15. To create a 'previous event' to trigger the sound, select the **Sandcastle** picture on the slide. Select **Fly In** animation.

16. Click [Animation Pane] to display the task pane at the right of the screen. **Picture 21** appears in the order area.

17. Click the **Move Up** button, 🔼, from **Re-Order** so that it occurs before the sound. Run the slide show. The sound will play 5 seconds after that image is animated. Notice that the sound icon is no longer displayed.

18. With **Picture 21** still selected, click the drop down arrow and select **Timing**.

19. From **Start**, select **After Previous** (which is after the slide opening).

20. Change the **Delay** to 4 seconds.

21. Click **OK** to apply the settings.

22. Select **Slide Show** then **From Current Slide**. The slide appears without the sandcastle image. After 4 seconds the image flies in, and after a further 5 seconds the sound will play. Notice that the sound icon is no longer displayed on the slide.

ℹ️ *Sounds can be previewed by clicking the **Play/Pause** button on the slide or by clicking the **Play** button found in the **Preview** group of the **Audio Tools Playback** tab.*

23. Press <Esc> to end the show.

24. Save the presentation as **Holiday Choice2**.

25. Leave it open for the next Driving Lesson.

Driving Lesson 34 - Inserting Movies

▣ Park and Read

Movies are also easily added to slides.

↱ Manoeuvres

1. Insert a new **Title Only** slide at the end of the **Holiday Choice2** presentation.

2. Add the title **Brought to you by**.

3. To insert a video clip, select the **Insert** tab, click the drop down arrow on **Video** from the **Media** group. Select **Video from File**.

4. Locate the data folder, select the **cia** video clip and click **Insert**.

5. With the video clip selected, display the **Video Tools Playback** tab. Note that the **Start** option is set to **On Click**.

6. Display the **Slide Show** tab and select **From Current Slide** button to view the current slide in action. Click on the **CiA** icon to start the movie.

7. Press **<Esc>** when it is finished to end the show.

8. To change the movie so that it plays automatically, select the movie object on the slide, then display the **Video Tools Playback** tab.

9. Change the **Start** option to **Automatically** from the **Video Options** group.

10. View the slide show for this slide again. The movie starts when the slide opens. Press **<Esc>** when it is finished to end the show.

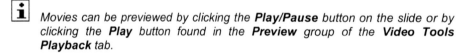

*Movies can be previewed by clicking the **Play/Pause** button on the slide or by clicking the **Play** button found in the **Preview** group of the **Video Tools Playback** tab.*

11. Leave the presentation open for the next Driving Lesson.

Driving Lesson 35 - Introducing Animation

🅿 Park and Read

It has been seen that different items on a slide can be animated. Items can be introduced with a click of the mouse, or automatically after a specified time.

ℝ Manoeuvres

1. Using the **Holiday Choice2** presentation, move to slide **1** and make sure the **Animation Pane** is displayed.

2. Select the title text box and apply the entrance effect **Wedge** from the **Animation** group on the **Animations** tab (click **More Entrance Effects** if it is not displayed).

ℹ️ *Recently used effects will appear in the **Entrance** shortcut menu. Effects that have not been used recently can be located in **More Entrance Effects**.*

3. Make sure **Start** shows **On Click**.

4. Now select the picture and add the entrance effect of **Pinwheel**.

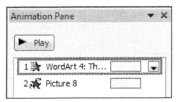

5. From the task pane, select the entry for **WordArt 4** and click the drop down arrow.

6. Choose **Effect Options** and from the **Sound** drop down list select **Drum Roll**. Click **OK**.

7. In the same way, apply the sound **Laser** to the next object, **Picture 8**.

8. View the slide show. Click to display the text and click again to reveal the picture, then end the show.

9. Apply timing, to start **After Previous** with a delay of **4** seconds, to both objects.

10. View the show again and notice the time delay between the animations and sounds.

11. End the show, but leave the presentation open.

Driving Lesson 36 - Animation Sequences

🄿 Park and Read

The order in which animated objects are introduced to the slide can be changed. What happens after they are animated can also be specified.

🄿 Manoeuvres

1. View slide **1** of the **Holiday Choice2** presentation in **Normal View**.

2. To apply the picture's animation first, from the **Animation Pane**, select **Picture 8** and click the **Re-Order Up** button, 🔼.

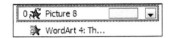

3. View the slide show for the first slide and notice how the picture now appears first.

4. End the show.

5. Use the **Re-Order Down** button 🔽, to change the animation sequence back to how it was originally.

6. Save the changes to the presentation and close it.

7. Open the **Kittens** presentation and display slide **2**.

8. Use **Shapes** on the **Insert** tab to draw a small smiley face at the left of the title text and colour it yellow.

9. Click in the bulleted list on the left of the slide to select it and from the **Animations** tab, apply the **Entrance** effect **Fly In**.

10. Select ⬚ 1 ★ Rectangle 3: F... ⬚   ▾ , click the drop down arrow and select **Effect Options**.

ℹ️ *If **Rectangle 3** is replaced in the **Animation Pane** by its three component lines, click the chevrons, ⬚ ⌃ ⬚ , to collapse the display.*

11. From the **Effect** tab in the **Fly In** dialog box, display the drop down list for **Direction** in the **Settings** area. Look at the options and select **From Left**.

12. Display the drop down list for **Animate text** to see the options. Leave the selection as **All at once**.

continued over

Driving Lesson 36 - Continued

13. To change the appearance of the bulleted points after they have been animated, display the **After animation** drop down list and select a **Red** colour (you may have to find it from **More Colours** then click **OK**).

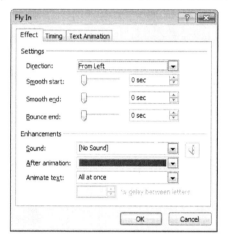

14. Click **OK** to close the dialog box.

15. Apply the same settings to the second bulleted list, but set it to fly in from the right.

16. Select the smiley face and apply the **Entrance** effect **Pinwheel**. Apply an **After animation** effect of **Hide on Next Mouse Click** to the object.

17. To change the sequence of the animation effects just applied, in the **Animation Pane**, move the smiley face up to the top of the list.

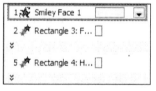

18. View the slide show for slide 2 only, clicking the mouse to view the effects. The slide will appear with only the title and the cat image displayed. The first click will introduce the yellow face. At the next click the face will disappear, and the first bulleted text point will appear. As the mouse is repeatedly clicked, each item of text in the two bulleted lists will turn red as the next is displayed.

*To remove an animation effect, click on the drop down arrow for the effect in the **Animation Pane** and select **Remove**.*

19. End the show and close the presentation <u>without</u> saving.

Driving Lesson 37 - Revision

This is not an ECDL test. Testing may only be carried out through certified ECDL test centres. This covers the features introduced in this section. Try not to refer to the preceding Driving Lessons while completing it.

1. Open the presentation **Assessment**.

2. View slide **4** in **Normal View**.

3. View the **Animation Pane**.

4. Select each of the Jigsaw Piece images in turn (from **Open** to **Pictures**) and apply a different **Entrance** animation effect to each one. Each image is to be animated to **Start after Previous** with a delay of **2** seconds.

5. Change the animation order for the nine Jigsaw Piece images so that they appear in a more random sequence.

6. View the slide show for this slide.

7. Close the presentation <u>without</u> saving.

If you experienced any difficulty completing this Revision refer back to the Driving Lessons in this section. Then redo the Revision.

Driving Lesson 38 - Revision

This is not an ECDL test. Testing may only be carried out through certified ECDL test centres. This covers the features introduced in this section. Try not to refer to the preceding Driving Lessons while completing it.

1.   Open the presentation **Kittens**.

2.   On slide **1** apply an **Entrance** animation effect of **Zoom** to the picture of the cat (**Picture 4**).

3.   Insert the **Growl** sound from the supplied data files as a separate item.

4.   Set the sound up to play **automatically**, **4** seconds after the previous event (that is 4 seconds after the cat image appears).

5.   View the slide show for slide **1** to hear the sound.

6.   Close the presentation without saving.

If you experienced any difficulty completing this Revision refer back to the Driving Lessons in this section. Then redo the Revision.

Once you are confident with the features, complete the Record of Achievement Matrix referring to the section at the end of the guide. Only when competent move on to the next Section.

Section 5
Slide Shows

By the end of this Section you should be able to:

Create and Edit Action Buttons/Hyperlinks

Create and Edit Custom Shows

Run a Custom Show

Apply Slide Transitions

Apply Timings

Set up a Slide Show

Use Various Techniques while Running a Show

To gain an understanding of the above features, work through the **Driving Lessons** in this **Section**.

For each **Driving Lesson**, read the **Park and Read** instructions, without touching the keyboard, then work through the numbered steps of the **Manoeuvres** on the computer. Complete the **Revision Exercise(s)** at the end of the section to test your knowledge.

Driving Lesson 39 - Action Buttons

▣ Park and Read

Action buttons can be added to allow rapid and easy navigation between slides during the presentation using **hyperlinks**. Action buttons also allow movement to other presentations, files, web sites and various other destinations.

Manoeuvres

1. Open the **Training** presentation and save it as **Training2**.

2. Select slide **4, The Open Learning Guide**.

3. To create an action button that links to slide **7**, click the **Shapes** button on the **Home** tab, look in the **Action Buttons** section of the list and select the **Information** action button, .

4. Click and drag the shape of the button on the bottom left side of the slide.

 *If a message appears about saving the presentation, select **Yes**.*

5. The **Action Settings** dialog box appears. Ensure that the **Mouse Click** tab is selected. Click the **Hyperlink to** option, scroll down the drop down list and select **Slide....**

6. A list of slides in the presentation is displayed, select slide **7 Where to Get More Information**.

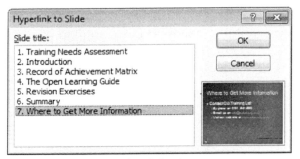

7. Click **OK**, and then **OK** to close the dialog box.

8. Click the **Slide Show** tab and select **From Current Slide** to see the slide as it will appear in the presentation.

9. When the cursor appears, click the action button. The presentation moves to the **Where to Get More Information** slide.

continued over

Driving Lesson 39 - Continued

10. The presentation will continue from its new position (there is no automatic return to the original slide). Click until the show is ended.

11. With slide **7** displayed in **Normal View**, draw a **Custom** action button, , which will link to a separate presentation.

12. In the **Action Settings** dialog box, select **Hyperlink to** and then **Other PowerPoint Presentation**.

13. Select **CIA Seminar** from the list.

14. Click **OK** and ensure **Hyperlink to Slide** shows **Slide 1** highlighted and then click **OK**.

15. Click **OK** to create the link and with the button selected type **CiA** so it is labelled.

16. View the slide show and test the button. Click to view the **CIA** show. End the **CIA** show to return to the **Training2** show.

17. Press <**Esc**> to end that show and return to **Normal View**.

18. At the bottom left of slide **5** draw a **Document** action button, . This will link to a *Word* document.

19. From **Action Settings** select **Hyperlink to** then **Other File**.

20. Choose the **Sample** file and click **OK** then **OK** again.

21. Add the text **Sample** to the button. Enlarge the button if necessary.

22. Run the show and after the text has loaded click the **Sample** action button. *Word* starts and opens the document. Close *Word*, without saving if prompted and end the show.

23. Right click on the **Sample** button and select **Edit Hyperlink**. To remove the hyperlink from an action button, select **None** from **Action on click** and click **OK**.

 *Alternatively, right click on the button and select **Remove Hyperlink**.*

24. Hyperlinks can also be applied to text or graphical objects - you don't always have to use action buttons. Display slide **7** and select the text **Information**.

continued over

Driving Lesson 39 - Continued

25. Display the **Insert** tab and click the **Hyperlink** button from the **Links** group.

26. Make sure **Existing File or Web Page** is selected on the left and type **www.ciatraining.co.uk** in the **Address** box. *PowerPoint* adds the necessary components to make this a valid web address.

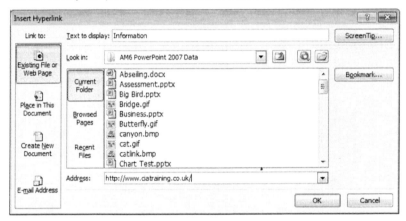

27. Click **OK**. The text **Information** is displayed in a different colour to indicate it is a hyperlink.

28. Run the show from slide **7**. Move the cursor over the **Information** text. The cursor changes to a hand.

29. Click on the text. If an Internet connection exists, your browser application will start and the **CiA Training** home page will be displayed.

30. Close the browser window and end the slide show.

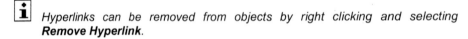

Hyperlinks can be removed from objects by right clicking and selecting **Remove Hyperlink**.

31. Save the presentation and leave it open.

Driving Lesson 40 - Editing an Action Button

▣ Park and Read

It is possible to change the destination of an action button or any hyperlink, after creating it. This may be necessary for example if a web address (**URL**) or a file location changes.

ℝ Manoeuvres

1. On slide **7** right click on the **CiA** action button, (take care not to click on the text content, you need to click part of the button itself).

2. Select **Edit Hyperlink**. The current hyperlink destination is shown.

3. To change the link to a different presentation, click the **Hyperlink to** drop down list.

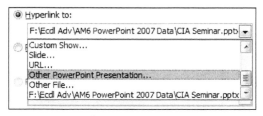

4. Click on **Other PowerPoint Presentation**.

5. Select the **Holiday Choice** presentation from the data files and click **OK**, then **OK** again to accept **Slide 1** as the destination of the link.

6. Click **OK** in the **Action Settings** dialog box.

7. View the slide show for this slide and when the text has loaded click the button to view the linked presentation.

8. End both shows.

9. On slide **7** right click on the word **Information**.

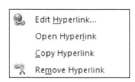

ⓘ *Notice there is an option here to **Remove** the hyperlinks from this text.*

10. Select **Edit Hyperlink**.

continued over

Driving Lesson 40 - Continued

11. Highlight the text in the **Address** box and type **www.ecdl.com**. Click **OK**.

12. Run the show from slide **7**. Click on the **Information** text. If a connection exists your browser application will start and the **ECDL** home page will be displayed.

 The appearance of the web page was correct at time of writing. It may change over time.

13. Close the browser window and end the slide show.

14. On slide **7**, right click on the **CiA** button and select **Remove Hyperlink**.

15. Run the show from slide **7**. Click on the **CiA** button text. The button no longer contains a hyperlink and there will be no action.

16. End the show.

17. Close the presentation <u>without</u> saving.

Driving Lesson 41 - Custom Shows

▣ Park and Read

Custom shows allow different parts of one presentation to be shown as different shows to different audiences without the need for creating multiple versions of the same presentation. For example, an audience of salespeople could see a presentation without seeing those slides relating to administration and training, and finance staff could be given the same presentation, but without the sales and training slides. A custom show can be set up so that certain slides can be missed out when necessary.

⌐ Manoeuvres

1. Open the **Business** presentation.

2. On the **Insert** tab, select **Header & Footer**, check the box to include **Slide number** and click **Apply to All**.

    Header & Footer

3. Save the presentation as **Custom**.

4. The presentation is to be shown to two departments of the same company: **Finance** and **Marketing**. To avoid the creation of two separate presentations, two custom shows are to be created, each showing a different selection of slides.

5. On the **Slide Show** tab, select **Custom Slide Show** then **Custom Shows** to display the **Custom Shows** dialog box. Click the **New** button to open the **Define Custom Show** dialog box.

6. Name the custom show **Finance** as this is the show to be given to that department.

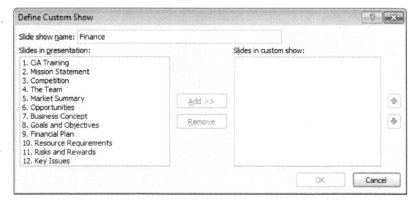

continued over

Driving Lesson 41 - Continued

7. The **Finance** people do not need to see all of the **Marketing** slides. Select the first slide, then click **Add**.

8. Select slide **2** and then hold down <Ctrl> as you select slides **4**, **9**, **11** and **12**. Click **Add** to add them to the custom show.

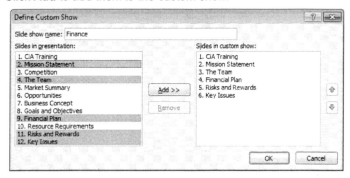

9. Click **OK** to return to the **Custom Shows** dialog box.

10. Create another custom show called **Marketing** (slides **1**, **2**, **3**, **4**, **6**, **7** and **12**). Click **OK**.

11. To edit the **Marketing** department's show, select **Marketing** from the list in the **Custom Shows** dialog box and click **Edit**.

12. Click on slide **6 Business Concept** at the right of the dialog box.

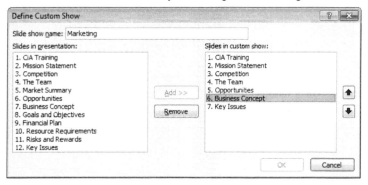

13. Click **Remove**.

14. Slide **4 The Team** is to be moved after **Opportunities**. Select slide **4** from the right of the dialog box.

15. Click **Move Down**, .

16. Click **OK** and then **Close**.

17. Save the presentation and leave it open.

Driving Lesson 42 - Running a Custom Show

▣ Park and Read

After custom shows have been created they can be run via the **Ribbon**, or more professionally by adding action buttons to the presentation.

⌒ Manoeuvres

1. View slide **1** of the **Custom** presentation in **Normal View**, display the **Slide Show** tab and click **Custom Slide Show**.

2. To run the **Finance** show, select it from the list.

3. Click the mouse to advance the slides, noting which slides are displayed, and click to exit.

4. View the **Marketing** show in the same way.

5. To create a copy of the **Marketing** show, click **Custom Slide Show** and select **Custom Shows**.

6. Select the **Marketing** show and click **Copy**.

7. The new show **Copy of Marketing** appears below the others. Click on it and select **Edit**.

8. Change the name to **Directors** and click **OK**.

9. A copy is not actually needed. Select **Directors** and click **Remove**. Close the **Custom Shows** dialog box.

continued over

Driving Lesson 42 - Continued

10. It would be better to select the required show by using action buttons on the first slide. Insert an **Action Button:Custom** at the lower left of slide **1**. The **Action Settings** dialog box is displayed.

11. Select **Hyperlink to** and from the list select **Custom Show | Finance** then click **OK** and **OK** again.

12. With the button selected type in **Finance**. Click away from the button.

13. Repeat the above steps to create a button for the **Marketing** custom show at the right of the first button.

14. Resize and move the buttons as necessary.

15. Because slide **1** will now always be displayed in order to start the custom shows, you may want to remove it from each show sequence. To remove slide **1**, click **Custom Slide Show**, and select **Custom Shows**.

16. Select the **Finance** show and click the **Edit** button.

17. Select slide **1** from the list on the right and click **Remove**. Click **OK**. Repeat these steps for the **Marketing** show and close the dialog box.

18. Run the full slide show, 12 slides will be displayed. Start the show again and use the **Finance** button to see the shortened custom show, advancing by clicking. This is easier than using the Ribbon. Notice the slide numbers at the bottom right of the slides.

19. Save the presentation and leave it open.

Driving Lesson 43 - Applying Transitions

▣ Park and Read

To add interest to a slide show, a transition can be applied to slides. This is a special effect, which controls how one slide changes to the next. Timings can be applied to the effects, so that they appear after a specified interval, or they can be displayed manually by clicking the mouse.

☞ Manoeuvres

1. In **Slide Sorter View**, select slide **1**.

2. To create a transition effect, display the **Transitions** tab, and click the **More** arrow in the **Transitions** gallery.

3. Select any effect from the list of transition effects shown. A demonstration of the effect is shown.

4. Try using some of the other effects to see what they do, then select **Dissolve**.

5. Change the **Duration** to 4 seconds using the up spinner, located in the **Timing** group.

6. In **Advance Slide** options, select **On Mouse Click**, then click **Apply To All**. All slides now have the **Dissolve** transition effect applied.

ℹ️ *Each slide can have a different effect if desired, although normally they would all be the same. To apply an individual effect, select the slide, choose an effect from the **Transition** to this **Slide Group**, but do not click **Apply to All**.*

7. Select the first slide, then view the slide show. Click the mouse button to move through all the slides and notice the effects as the slides change.

ℹ️ *A slide that has a transition applied has a symbol underneath it in **Slide Sorter** view.*

8. To apply timings to the transition effects select slide **1**.

9. At the moment slide transitions do not start until the mouse is clicked. Select the **Transitions** tab. Under **Advance Slide**, remove the check from **On Mouse Click**, then check **After**.

continued over

Driving Lesson 43 - Continued

10. Use the up spinner to increase the time to **5** seconds:

11. Click **Apply to All**. In **Slide Sorter View**, the transition timing for each slide is now shown underneath the slide image.

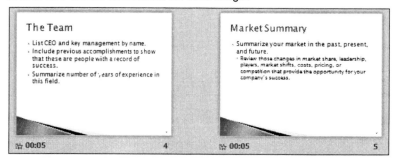

12. View the slide show. The slides advance every 5 seconds without the need for clicking. Using this option the slide show could be left to run without the need for a presenter, as a continuously running display for example.

13. When the show ends, remove the check from **After** and select **On Mouse Click** again. Click **Apply To All**. This has removed the transition timings.

*It is possible to select both **Advance Slide** options (mouse click and automatic) at the same time. Then each transition can be activated by using the mouse if required, but if this is not used within the set time, the transition will start automatically.*

14. Save the presentation and leave it open for the next exercise.

Driving Lesson 44 - Applying Timings

▣ Park and Read

Instead of applying timings to slide transitions, slide shows can also have timings applied to each slide separately. This means that enough time can be allowed to describe each particular slide. These timings are set up during a **Rehearsal**.

If a presentation contains hyperlinks and action buttons it should be run manually, so that the links can be used.

Manoeuvres

1. In **Slide Sorter View**, select the first slide. To apply timings select **Slide Show** tab and select **Rehearse Timings** from the **Set Up** group.

2. The slide show begins, with the **Rehearsal** dialog box on the screen.

3. Allow enough time to talk about the slide then click the **Next** button, ⬛. The next screen appears with the time for the current slide reset to zero.

4. Pause the rehearsal by clicking ⬛, then restart it by using the **Resume Recording** button. Move to the next slide/effect.

5. View the entire presentation, clicking the **Next** button after the required time period for each slide until finished.

6. At the end of the rehearsal a dialog box appears showing the total time for the slide show and asking if the timings are to be saved for future use.

    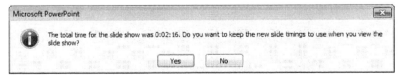

7. Click **Yes**. The individual times for each slide are now displayed. The total time for the slide show is made up of these times. The timings can be changed at any time by clicking the **Rehearse Timings** button again.

8. Individual timings can still be amended. Click on slide **3**. In the **Transitions** tab, increase the **Advance slide** time value by 5 seconds.

9. Save the presentation and leave it open.

Driving Lesson 45 - Setting up a Slide Show

▣ Park and Read

A slide show can be set up to run in a few different ways. It can be run manually, by clicking the mouse, or automatically using timings. It can also be set up to loop, running continuously. Note that even when timings have been applied to a show, you should check to make sure that it has been set up to use these timings.

⌒ Manoeuvres

1. To make sure the timings specified earlier are to be used when the show runs, display the **Slide Show** tab and select **Set Up Slide Show**.

2. In the **Set Up Show** dialog box under **Advance slides**, select the option **Using timings, if present**.

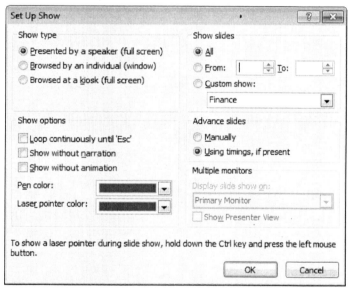

3. Click **OK**, then save the presentation. View the slide show, which will now play using the timings set in the rehearsal. There is no need to click the mouse.

4. Select the **Slide Show** tab and select **Set Up Slide Show**.

5. To disable the timings, select **Manually** under **Advance slides**. Click **OK**.

6. Click on the first slide and then view the show.

continued over

Driving Lesson 45 - Continued

7. The first slide in the presentation appears. Click the mouse to move to the second slide.

8. Move through the rest of the slide show.

9. At the end of the show change the set up within the **Set Up Show** dialog box to use timings again, but don't click **OK** yet (the show could still be advanced using the mouse if desired).

10. To make the show run continuously, check **Loop continuously until 'Esc'**.

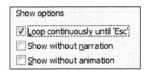

11. Click **OK**.

12. View the slide show again and when the end is reached, the show will start again.

13. Press **<Esc>** to end the slide show.

14. To stop the show looping, select **Set Up Slide Show** from the **Slide Show** tab and uncheck **Loop continuously....**

15. Click **OK**.

16. Save and close the presentation.

17. Open the presentation **Holiday Choice**.

18. Select the graphic on slide **1** and apply an **Entrance Animation** effect of **Fly In**.

19. Set **Direction** to **From Left** and use the **Timing** option so that it starts after the previous event with a delay of 3 seconds.

20. View the show for this slide only.

21. The show can also be run without animation. Select the **Slide Show** tab and click **Set Up Slide Show** button.

22. Under **Show options**, check **Show without animation** and click **OK**.

23. View the show for this slide again and notice how the picture is not animated.

24. Close the presentation <u>without</u> saving.

Driving Lesson 46 - Slide Show Techniques

P Park and Read

While running a show, you may need to pause to expand on a particular point, or indicate areas on a slide. There are various ways of controlling the show and being able to do just that.

↱ Manoeuvres

1. Open the presentation **Theatre**.

2. Display the **Slide Show** tab and start the slide show. Click to move to slide **2**. Right click on the screen to display a menu of options.

i *Some of these options are also available as buttons (almost hidden) in the lower left corner of the screen.*

3. From the shortcut menu, select **Pointer Options | Pen**. You are going to annotate the slide.

4. Click and drag to draw a line beneath **newly refurbished**. This method could be used to emphasise a point as the show is presented.

5. Right click and select **Pointer Options | Eraser**. Click with the eraser on the line to remove the pen mark.

6. Right click and select **Pointer Options | Arrow**, then click to advance to slide **3**. Slides will only advance when the **Arrow** option is active.

7. You may wish to pause for questions. So there are no distractions, press the <**B**> key to display a black screen (alternatively, right click and select **Screen | Black Screen**). Click or press any key to resume the show.

8. Press the <**W**> key to display a white screen (alternatively, right click and select **Screen | White Screen**).

9. Click or press any key to resume the show. To end the show at any time either press <**Esc**> or right click and select **End Show**.

10. Apply a transition effect of your choice to all slides, with automatic timing of **5** seconds.

11. When timings are applied the show can be paused during its progress. Start the slide show and let it continue to slide **3**.

12. Right click and select **Pause** to pause the show.

13. Right click again and select **Resume** to start it again. Let the show continue to the end and the click to exit.

14. Close the presentation <u>without</u> saving.

Driving Lesson 47 - Revision

This is not an ECDL test. Testing may only be carried out through certified ECDL test centres. This covers the features introduced in this section. Try not to refer to the preceding Driving Lessons while completing it.

1. Open the **Kittens** presentation.

2. Create a custom show called **Information** consisting of slides **3**, **4**, **5** and **8**.

3. Create a second custom show called **Charity** consisting of slides **2**, **6** and **7**.

4. Create an action button for each custom show on slide **1**, one at the bottom left of the slide and one at the bottom right.

5. View the slide show from slide **1** and use the action buttons to view each custom show in turn.

6. Use the **Pen** option to draw on slide **2** in the **Charity** custom show - underline **How to make a donation**.

7. Change back to the **Arrow** pointer option.

8. Pause the show by displaying a black screen, then restart it.

9. End the slide show. A message will ask if you want to keep your ink annotations, click **Discard**.

10. Save the presentation as **Shelter** and close it.

If you experienced any difficulty completing this Revision refer back to the Driving Lessons in this section. Then redo the Revision.

Driving Lesson 48 - Revision

This is not an ECDL test. Testing may only be carried out through certified ECDL test centres. This covers the features introduced in this section. Try not to refer to the preceding Driving Lessons while completing it.

1.   Open the presentation **CIA Seminar**.

2.   Apply a **Cover** slide transition to all slides.

3.   All transitions should be advanced **automatically** after **5** seconds, but also leave the **On Mouse Click** option selected.

4.   Set the **Transition Duration** to **4 seconds**.

5.   Set up the show to use timings and to lcop continuously.

6.   View the slide show. Use the mouse button on a few slides to override the timings and display a black screen while viewing slide **3**.

7.   Continue the show.

8.   After it starts for the second time press **<Esc>**.

9.   Remove the option to loop continuously.

10. Rehearse timings for the show, advancing slide **1** after about **10** seconds and all others after about **15** seconds.

11. Keep the timings.

12. Save the presentation as **Seminar Complete**.

13. View the slide show again.

14. 'Close the presentation.

If you experienced any difficulty completing this Revision refer back to the Driving Lessons in this section. Then redo the Revision.

Once you are confident with the features, complete the Record of Achievement Matrix referring to the section at the end of the guide.

Section 6
Linking

By the end of this Section you should be able to:

Create a Link to a Text File

Link to a Chart and a Worksheet Range

Link an Image to a File

Modify Linked Data

Break Links and Embed Objects

Edit and Delete Embedded Data

Save a Slide as an Image

To gain an understanding of the above features, work through the **Driving Lessons** in this **Section**.

For each **Driving Lesson**, read the **Park and Read** instructions, without touching the keyboard, then work through the numbered steps of the **Manoeuvres** on the computer. Complete the **Revision Exercise(s)** at the end of the section to test your knowledge.

Driving Lesson 49 - Embedding

▣ Park and Read

Objects can be embedded on a slide. This means that a copy of the data is actually stored with the slide and can be edited from the slide. If the source data changes, or is deleted, the data on the slide will be unaffected.

↱ Manoeuvres

1. Open the **Kittens** presentation and save it as **Links**.

2. At the end of the presentation create a new **Title Only** slide and add the title **Embedded Text**.

3. To insert data, on the **Insert** tab choose **Object** from the **Text** group, then **Create from file** option.

4. Click **Browse** and locate the supplied data files. Select the **Labradors** file and click **OK**.

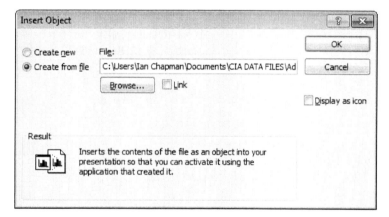

5. Click **OK** to embed the text file.

6. With the embedded text still selected (within a frame), press **<Delete>** to remove the data from the slide.

7. Repeat steps **3 – 5** to embed the data again.

8. To edit the data, double click the text on the slide. The embedded text is opened in editing view. Select the heading **Our Sanctuary** and underline it.

9. Click on a blank area of the slide to close the editing view.

10. Save the presentation (as **Links**) and leave it open.

Driving Lesson 50 - Linking Text

🅿 Park and Read

Objects on a slide can be **linked** to external data from a variety of other applications. Linking an object means that the data is not actually stored with the slide and the source data can be opened directly from *PowerPoint*. If the source data changes, the changes can be reflected automatically on the slide. If the source data is deleted, the text will no longer be available in the slide.

⌒ Manoeuvres

1. At the end of the **Links** presentation, create a new **Title Only** slide and add the title **Linked Text**.

2. To create the link, on the **Insert** tab choose **Object** from the **Text** group, then **Create from file** option.

3. Click **Browse** and locate the data files. Select the **Labradors** file.

4. Click **OK** and in the **Insert Object** dialog box, check **Link**.

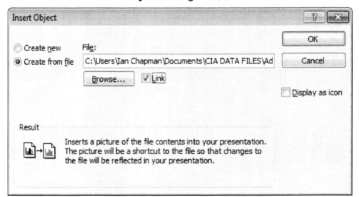

ℹ️ *If **Display as icon** is checked, the text will be displayed on the slide as an icon. In **Normal View**, double clicking the icon will open the source object. In a slide show, this text cannot be accessed.*

5. Click **OK** to insert the linked object and then save the presentation.

6. To edit the document, double click the text on the slide. *Word* starts and opens the original source document.

7. Select the heading **Our Sanctuary** and make it italic. Save the **Labradors** document and close *Word*. Notice the change is now shown on the **Linked Text** slide, but not on the **Embedded Text** slide.

8. Leave the presentation open.

Driving Lesson 51 - Linking to a Chart

▣ Park and Read

Data can be imported into *PowerPoint* from spreadsheets. Rather than create a chart from scratch, if a suitable one already exists within a workbook you can create a link to it.

⌐ Manoeuvres

1.   At the end of the **Links** presentation, create a new **Title Only** slide and add the title **Linked Chart**.

2.   Start *Excel* and open the workbook **Numbers** from the data files.

3.   With the **Admittances** sheet tab selected, click on the chart to select it then click **Copy**, ⬚, from the **Home** tab.

4.   Use the **Taskbar** to return to *PowerPoint*.

5.   To insert the link to the chart, display the **Home** tab, select the **Paste** drop down list and select **Paste Special**.

6.   Select the **Paste link** option.

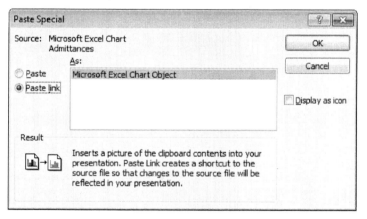

7.   Click **OK** to paste the linked chart on to the slide. Resize if necessary.

8.   Double click the chart to open the original in *Excel*.

9.   Close *Excel*.

10. Save the presentation and leave *PowerPoint* open.

Driving Lesson 52 - Linking to a Worksheet Range

▣ Park and Read

A link can be created from a slide to a specific range of data on a worksheet.

↱ Manoeuvres

1. At the end of the **Links** presentation create a new **Title Only** slide and add the title **Linked Range**.

2. Open *Excel* and display the **Numbers** workbook.

3. At the bottom of the screen, select the **Data** tab.

4. Click and drag to select the range **B3:D15**.

5. Click the **Copy** button, ⬜.

6. Switch back to *PowerPoint*.

7. To link to the range, click the **Home** tab, select the **Paste** drop down list and select **Paste Special**.

8. Select the **Paste link** option and click **OK**.

ℹ️ *To embed a range, select the basic **Paste** function. The figures would not then be updated if the source worksheet is changed.*

9. The range selected from the spreadsheet is now linked to the presentation.

10. Enlarge the range object by dragging a corner handle then save the presentation.

11. Leave *Excel* and the presentation open.

Driving Lesson 53 - Linking to an Image File

▣ Park and Read

Images can also be linked in a presentation. They can be linked using **Insert Picture from file** or **Insert Object**. If the original image is edited in any way, the changes are reflected in the linked *PowerPoint* object.

⌒ Manoeuvres

1. At the end of the **Links** presentation create another **Title Only** slide and name it **Linked Image**.

2. To create a link to an image file, select the **Insert** tab and click the **Object** button.

3. Check **Create from file**, click **Browse** and select **catlink.bmp** from the data files. Click **OK**.

4. Check **Link**.

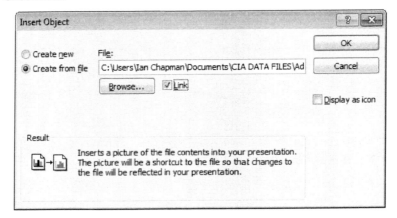

5. Click **OK** to insert the linked object.

ⓘ *It may be necessary to use a different method to create links to other types of image file, i.e. Click **Picture** from the **Insert** tab, select the image file, click the drop down arrow on the **Insert** button and select **Link to File**. An image linked in this way will appear in the **Links** dialog box, see Driving Lesson 55, but will always be updated manually.*

6. The linked image can be manipulated like any inserted object. Enlarge the image slightly and position it in the centre of the slide.

7. Save the presentation and close.

Driving Lesson 54 - Modifying Linked Data

P Park and Read

Whenever a presentation containing links is opened, you will always be prompted to update the links. If the option is accepted, all linked objects within the presentation will be updated with the current versions from the source data. If not, they will be left unchanged.

Manoeuvres

1.   If the *Excel* spreadsheet **Numbers** is not open, open it and select the worksheet **Data**.

2.   Change the **March** figure for **Healthy Cats** to **20**.

3.   Select the worksheet **Admittances** and right click any data series for **Healthy Cats** (the lighter colour).

4.   Select **Format Data Series** and select **Fill**.

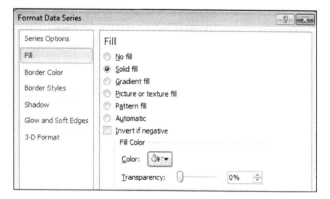

5.   Choose yellow from the **Color** selector then click **Close**.

6.   Save the spreadsheet and close *Excel*.

7.   Open *Word* and open the document **Labradors**. Add the text 'This shelter is now closed.' after the first paragraph.

8.   Save the document with the same name and close *Word*.

9.   Open *Microsoft Paint*, (**Start** button, **All Programs, Accessories, Paint**) and open the image **catlink** from the supplied data files.

10. Use the **Fill with Color** tool , to change its colour from black to yellow.

11. Save the image and close the application.

continued over

Driving Lesson 54 - Continued

12. In *PowerPoint* open the presentation **Links** - the following prompt appears:

13. Click **Update Links**.

14. View slide **9 Embedded Text** to see that the text is unchanged.

15. View slide **10 Linked Text** to see that the text added in *Word* has also been changed in *PowerPoint*.

16. View slide **11 Linked Chart** to see that the data series changed to yellow in *Excel* has also been changed in *PowerPoint*.

17. View slide **12 Linked Range** to see the amended March figure for **Healthy Cats** in the table.

18. View slide **13 Linked Image** to see that the change in image colour is also shown in *PowerPoint*.

19. Save the presentation.

20. Leave it open for the next Driving Lesson.

Driving Lesson 55 - Managing Links

🅿 Park and Read

All the links in a presentation can be managed from the **Links** dialog box. Links can be updated manually and changed so that they can only be updated from here. They can also be broken or changed to a different location.

⤴ Manoeuvres

1. In the **Links** presentation, click the **File** tab. On the bottom right side of the **Info** screen click **Edit Links to Files**.

2. Select the **Document** link and click the **Manual** option at the bottom of the dialog box. The file is still linked, but will only ever be updated when manually triggered from this dialog box.

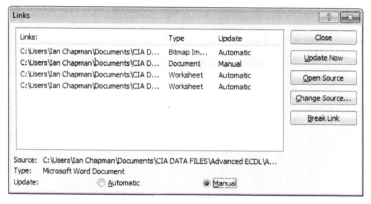

3. To update the document link, select it and click **Update Now**. All current changes in the **Labradors** document will immediately be reflected in the presentation.

4. To break the link to the chart, make sure the **Chart** link (to the **Admittances** sheet) is selected. Move the cursor over the links to see the full path.

5. Click **Break Link**. Any changes to the original chart in the **Numbers** spreadsheet will now <u>not</u> be reflected in the presentation.

ℹ️ *Change Source is usually used to change the link path when the source document has been moved to a new location.*

6. Click **Close** to close the **Links** dialog box. Select slide **11**, **Linked Chart** and double click on the chart. It is now a fixed picture and no longer linked to a spreadsheet.

7. Save and close the presentation.

Driving Lesson 56 - Saving a Slide as an Image

▣ Park and Read

As well as using objects in slides, slides themselves can be used as objects within other applications. The easiest way to do this is to save the slide as an image file. This can then be manipulated using image processing programs and inserted into other applications such as *Word* or *Access,* or used in web pages.

⌒ Manoeuvres

1. Open the presentation **CIA Seminar** and display slide **3**, the organisation chart, in **Normal View**.

2. Click the **File** tab and select **Save As**.

3. Select the location of the supplied data files, enter a **File name** of **Organisation**, and click the drop down arrow in the **Save as type** box.

4. There are options to save the slide as an image file, including **GIF**, **JPEG** or **Bitmap** file formats. Select **GIF Graphics Interchange Format** (may be shown as just **GIF**, or similar).

5. Click **Save**. There is a prompt to export all slides in the presentation. Click **Current Slide Only** to save only the selected slide.

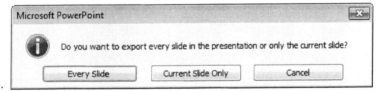

ℹ️ *If all slides are saved, they will be saved as individual images within a folder.*

6. Close the presentation and open *Word*.

7. On a new blank document type the line **Here is our new company structure**.

8. Use **Insert Picture** to insert the newly created **Organisation.gif** file under the text line.

9. Resize the image to half its size by dragging one of the corner handles.

10. Display the **Page Layout** tab and click the drop down arrow on the **Position** button in **Arrange**. Select **Position in Middle Center with Square Text Wrapping**.

11. Save the document as **New Structure** and close *Word*.

Driving Lesson 57 - Revision

This is not an ECDL test. Testing may only be carried out through certified ECDL test centres. This covers the features introduced in this section. Try not to refer to the preceding Driving Lessons while completing it.

1.   Open the presentation **Holiday Choice** and save it as **Revision57**.

2.   Create a **Title Only** slide at the end of the presentation.

3.   Enter the title **More Information Below**.

4.   Create a link to the *Word* document **Abseiling** from the data files.

5.   Reduce the size of the object until the title is not obscured.

6.   After this slide, insert another **Title Only** slide.

7.   Enter the title **You'll be abseiling here**.

8.   Insert the **canyon** image, as a linked object on this slide.

9.   Resize the graphic until it is double its original size.

10.   Move the graphic to the centre of the slide.

11.   View the slide show.

12.   Save **Slide 2** as a **JPEG** image file, called **Beach.jpg**.

13.   Save the changes to the presentation.

14.   Close the presentation.

If you experienced any difficulty completing this Revision refer back to the Driving Lessons in this section. Then redo the Revision.

Driving Lesson 58 - Revision

This is not an ECDL test. Testing may only be carried out through certified ECDL test centres. This covers the features introduced in this section. Try not to refer to the preceding Driving Lessons while completing it.

1. Create a new, blank presentation with a **Title Slide**.

2. Enter the title **World Rainfall** and click where indicated to add the subtitle **An Interesting Presentation**.

3. Insert a new **Title Only** slide with the title **London**.

4. Open the *Excel* workbook **Wet**. Copy the **London Rainfall** chart and paste it as a link into the **London** slide. Do not display the chart as an icon.

5. After slide **2** in the presentation, create another **Title Only** slide named **Mumbai**.

6. Paste the **Mumbai Rainfall** chart as a link into the new slide.

7. Save the presentation as **Linked Rainfall** and close it.

8. In *Excel*, select the **Data** sheet in the workbook **Wet**.

9. Mumbai's monsoon lasted into October. Change the appropriate **Rainfall** figure to **20**.

10. Change the colour of the **Mumbai Rainfall** data series to **Green**.

11. Change the colour of the data series in the **London Rainfall** chart to **Red**.

12. Save the workbook and close *Excel*.

13. Open the presentation **Linked Rainfall**, selecting to update the links when prompted.

14. Check that the charts reflect all the latest changes made to the workbook.

15. Embed the charts by breaking all links.

16. Save the presentation and then close it.

If you experienced any difficulty completing this Revision refer back to the Driving Lessons in this section. Then redo the Revision.

Once you are confident with the features, complete the Record of Achievement Matrix referring to the section at the end of the guide.

Answers

Driving Lesson 11

Step 1   A presentation can be viewed on screen, on an overhead projector, on 35mm slides or as web pages.

Step 2   No, because you must take into account the background, age, occupation and previous knowledge of each audience and tailor the presentation to their needs.

Step 3   Too many colours may distract the audience from the point of the slide.

Step 4   Colour combinations must be chosen carefully as some may be difficult for people with colour blindness to see. Using dark text on a dark background, or light text on a light background, may also cause problems.

Step 5   Colour gradients, patterns, textures and pictures can be used as background effects.

Step 8   No, the new slide is automatically converted to the design of the existing presentation.

Driving Lesson 23

Step 11   Parts of the image could now be re-coloured if desired.

Glossary

Action Button　　A button placed on a slide that can have actions attached such as navigating to another slide, or presentation, opening another application or playing a sound clip.

Animation　　Allows the appearance, movement and sound effects attached to any slide object to be specified and customised.

Arrange　　To position overlapping objects in relation to each other. They can be brought forward or sent backward, or placed on the top or bottom of the pile.

Chart Effects　　Custom animations that are specific to elements within a chart.

Colour Scheme　　A set of pre-defined colours applied to specific areas of a slide.

Combination Chart　　A chart which shows different types of information by using two or more chart types. Sometimes called a mixed chart.

Convert　　To change the nature of certain graphic images so that they become the same as drawn objects. Done by ungrouping and then grouping a single, selected picture. This cannot be done to bitmap images.

Cropping　　A process which allows only a selected part of an image to be displayed.

Custom Show　　A subset of slides within a show that can be created to be relevant to a specific target audience.

Design Template　　A pre-set design, including colours and fonts, that can be applied to slides.

Drawing Objects　　Objects that can be created directly on the slide using tools on the **Drawing** Toolbar.

Embedded Object　　An object on a slide is described as embedded if it is not linked to a source file.

Flip　　To create a mirror-image of an object around its horizontal or vertical axis.

Flowchart　　A diagram using pre-set **AutoShapes** to illustrate systems, processes or procedures.

Group　　To place two or more selected objects into a group, which is then treated as a single object.

Hyperlink　　A link attached to a selected object or piece of text that when clicked in **Slide Show** view, navigates to another location within the same slide, a different slide, a different presentation or application. Hyperlinks can also be attached to e-mail or web site addresses.

Linking

Data from external sources (e.g. text, data, charts etc.) can be linked (different from hyperlinking) to *PowerPoint* slides so that any changes to the source data is automatically applied to the object on the slide.

Mixed Chart

See combination chart.

Position

A setting available within the **Format** dialog box for any object, that allows its precise position to be specified as a pair of measurements from either the top left or centre of the slide.

Presentation

A collection of slides used by a speaker as a visual aid.

Save as an Image

An entire presentation, or the currently selected slide within a presentation, can be saved as a graphic image to be used as an object within other applications.

Shapes

Ready-made shapes in a variety of categories, which are available from a menu.

Slide Layout

The type of slide specified; e.g. **Bulleted List**, **Title Only** etc.

Slide Master

A view that is used to specify settings/formatting and/or add objects that will appear on every slide except the **Title Master**.

Slide Show

A presentation being run on screen, with all effects, transitions, sounds, etc.

Template

A presentation framework containing formatting, saved so that it can be used as the basis for future presentations.

Title Master

A view that is used to specify settings/formatting and/or add objects that will appear on every slide which is based on the **Title Slide** layout.

Transitions

Special effects that occur as one slide changes to the next during a **Slide Show**. Timings and sound effects may be specified as well as visual effects.

Ungroup

To return a previously grouped set of objects back to acting as individual objects.

Views

Different ways of looking at the slides within a presentation.

Index

Record of Achievement Matrix

This Matrix is to be used to measure your progress while working through the guide. This is a learning reinforcement process, you judge when you are competent.

Tick boxes are provided for each feature. 1 is for no knowledge, 2 some knowledge and 3 is for competent. A section is only complete when column 3 is completed for all parts of the section.

For details on sitting ECDL Examinations in your country please contact the local ECDL Licensee or visit the European Computer Driving Licence Foundation Limited web site at http://www.ecdl.org.

Tick the Relevant Boxes **1**: No Knowledge   **2**: Some Knowledge   **3**: Competent

Section	No	Driving Lesson	1	2	3
1 Preparation	1	Design Considerations			
	2	Colour Schemes & Accessibility			
	3	Background Effects			
	4	The Slide Master			
	5	Bullet Levels			
	6	The Title Master			
	7	Creating a Template			
	8	Using a Template			
	9	Inserting Text			
	10	Inserting Slides			
2 Images & Drawn Objects	13	Drawing Objects			
	14	Object Backgrounds			
	15	Rotating or Flipping Objects			
	16	Recolouring Pictures			
	17	Converting Pictures			
	18	Background Graphics			
	19	Arranging Objects			
	20	Cropping Images			
	21	Editing Images			
	22	Different Image Formats			
3 Charts	25	Combination Charts			
	26	Editing Charts			
	27	Animating Charts			
	28	Creating a Flowchart			
	29	Amending a Flowchart			
	30	Creating Other Diagrams			
4 Multimedia	33	Inserting Sounds			
	34	Inserting Movies			
	35	Introducing Animation			
	36	Animation Sequences			

Tick the Relevant Boxes   1: No Knowledge   2: Some Knowledge   3: Competent

Section	No	Driving Lesson	1	2	3
5 Slide Shows	39	Action Buttons			
	40	Editing an Action Button			
	41	Custom Shows			
	42	Running a Custom Show			
	43	Applying Transitions			
	44	Applying Timings			
	45	Setting up a Slide Show			
	46	Slide Show Techniques			
6 Linking	49	Embedding			
	50	Linking Text			
	51	Linking to a Chart			
	52	Linking to a Worksheet Range			
	53	Linking to an Image File			
	54	Modifying Linked Data			
	55	Managing Links			
	56	Saving a Slide as an Image			

Other Products from CiA Training

CiA Training is a leading publishing company which has consistently delivered the highest quality products since 1985. Our experienced in-house publishing team has developed a wide range of flexible and easy to use self-teach resources for individual learners and corporate clients all over the world.

At the time of publication, we currently offer approved ECDL materials for:

- **ECDL Syllabus 5.0**

- **ECDL Syllabus 5.0 Revision Series**

- **ECDL Advanced Syllabus 2.0**

- **ECDL Advanced Syllabus 2.0 Revision Series**

Previous syllabus versions are also available upon request.

We hope you have enjoyed using this guide and would love to hear your opinions about our materials. To let us know how we're doing, and to get up to the minute information on our current range of products, please visit us at:

www.ciatraining.co.uk